For Betty~

I love You!!

Thank You for being a
part of my life.

Carol
Thu Injaychock

Matters of the Heart:
A Cancer Journey

Dedication

This book is dedicated to...

Jan Parler, one of several mentors. Jan had been a survivor of breast cancer for three years prior to my diagnosis. We celebrated the end of my treatments only for her cancer to return and take her from this life way too soon.

Virginia Radford, who, when I was a teenage girl, showed me how to smile in spite of a cruel diagnosis. A smile she maintained for many years of treatments, until she no longer smiled on earth, but continues to smile in my heart.

Meg Turner and the support group at Carolinas Medical Center. Without you, I would have drowned in the emotional abyss of cancer.

Friends and family, mentioned and not mentioned in the pages that follow, who loved me through the year of hell.

My husband, Tom, and daughter, Lindsay Injaychock; my parents, Charles and Verna Fore; my sister, Cheryl Fore Longshore; and my brother, Gene Fore. A loving family makes an excellent suit of armor for fighting life's battles.

*"Give up to grace.
The ocean takes care of each wave
'til it gets to shore."*

Rumi

Table of Contents

Acknowledgements

My cancer journey generated a renewed interest in writing. Writing was a love of mine when I was young, but I had not written much of anything creative or personal since high school. During my cancer treatments, a kind friend, Carol Newman, delivered a writing journal for me to document my experience and for the first time in a long time, I began to write.

After the treatments were over and I had returned to work, a flier came across my desk advertising a local writing course. I did not sign up for the course, but I ordered the companion book entitled, *Spinning Words into Gold* by Maureen Ryan Griffin, a Charlotte, North Carolina writer and instructor. Six months or so later, I finally enrolled in a night course she taught at the local community college. That course turned into my attending a multitude of classes taught by Maureen, and a friendship ensued.

I wrote for the therapeutic feelings writing created within me. The writing prompts Maureen utilized began to slowly bring thoughts about my cancer experience to the surface, and the chapters in this book began to form. I came to think of my essays, and the dream of them becoming a book, as "my baby." Yet when all of the chapters were written, "my baby" needed some help. Things needed some re-arranging and Maureen introduced me to Amy Royal, a freelance editor. A breast cancer survivor herself, she took my baby and helped to put its parts in the proper tense and order. She also encouraged me to keep moving toward publishing, and it is because of her, that this book became a reality. "My baby" was born.

Without these two people in my life, my experience would

never have been anything more than writings in my journal; a journal I squirreled away after the treatments were over. A journal that rested on the top shelf of a closet in my bedroom for several years until I felt strong enough take it down and re-live the journey.

For these two wonderful midwives, I am eternally grateful.

"We are not human beings
having a spiritual experience.
We are spiritual beings
having a human experience."

Pierre Teilhard de Chardin

Introduction

As a young child, did you ever hang upside down from the top of the monkey bars? The world looked so different that way, and as exhilarating as it was, it also felt slightly unsettling. The ground so close to my head. The sky at my feet. I'd only last a few seconds before I wanted my life back the way it was supposed to be—upright, safe, and secure.

Sometimes our world turns upside down without warning. When no matter how hard we try, we can't seem to right ourselves; can't seem to get things back the way they're supposed to be. When we're forced to view our lives in a different way, sometimes for longer than what we think we can. For longer than we think we're able.

My world turned upside down nine years ago, when at the age of 44, I was diagnosed with breast cancer.

A cancer diagnosis is an emotional journey as well as a physical one. The emotional component, I believe, is the heavier weight and it's this aspect of the journey, the emotional one, where my story will focus. If you want to know what a certain medication does or about the latest treatment options, this isn't the book for you. This is spiritual, insightful, matters-of-the-heart stuff.

What you hold in your hands is a journey that embodies my faith, family, and career. It's my story as it happened—my journey and what I've learned from the experience. I'm not a writer by trade, nor am I a pastor or psychologist. I'm merely a daughter, sister, wife, mother and cancer survivor who has learned a lot about living life. Right side up AND upside down.

If you're a cancer patient new to diagnosis, I pray you will find hope, strength and support in these pages for what you are about to face. If you have a loved one going through this ordeal, I pray you will discover insight into what they might be feeling and find advice on what to say and do, or in some cases, what NOT to say and do.

To all who are reading this faith-based journey, I pray you might see life—if only for a little while—from a different view. That you may learn to trust that with God, you are more than able to handle life from any angle. Right side up, upside down, and everywhere in between.

Wishing you grace, hope, love, and peace -

Carol Fore Injaychock
Breast Cancer Survivor

***

I arrived in this world on a warm summer day in July 1958, born in southern California to Charles and Verna Fore, two very wonderful people. They welcomed me as their first daughter and younger sibling to their first-born son, Gene. Another daughter, Cheryl, would arrive two years later to complete our family.

From the onset, I was a Baptist by birthright and immediately welcomed into my parent's church as a new member of the "Cradle Roll." Starting Sunday morning by going to church as a family was as normal and routine as starting each day with breakfast.

My parents were originally from the western North Carolina area and believed the region to be the best place to raise their children. When I was six, we left California and moved to Asheville, North Carolina. Once we settled into our new home in the rural Erwin Hills section, my parents set about deciding which church to join. There were five or six Baptist churches close to our new house, but the one my parents were partial to was the one where my dad's maternal grandfather had been a founding member and pastor. This church, Victory Baptist, sat on a hill less than two miles away from our house. My Uncle Bob and Aunt Selma, who were like surrogate grandparents to my siblings and me, were already members there.

"It's a great church, Charlie," I overheard my Uncle Bob telling my dad in our kitchen one afternoon. It didn't take much arm twisting for my parents to decide, and just like that, Victory Baptist Church became our new church home.

Predictably, this church provided many opportunities to learn about God, and as a rural southern Baptist congregation, baptism by fear was the norm. The various ministers who preached to me during my youth informed me often that if I didn't profess my sins and commit my life to God, I would end up in hell. Sunday after Sunday, they repeated the same questions from the pulpit: "Where will you be in eternity—heaven or hell? Won't you today, make it right with God?"

So at the novice Christian age of eight, I dedicated my life to God and was baptized in the vestibule of that small church in its lifesaving waters. At the time, it was mostly a matter of the heart. It just "felt right." On a more practical front, I could see the benefits of ensuring I wouldn't end up in a fire pit called "Hell," and I felt certain I'd made a commitment to God that would protect me from harm; a commitment I would honor all the days of my life.

That event provided the foundation by which I began to build my faith. As I grew older, I continued to attend Sunday school, became a member of Acteens (a group of girls who came together like the Girl Scouts with a biblical slant to the activities), and I memorized multiple Bible verses. I learned many lessons during those formative years; for example, if I felt "lost" or unsure, how to open a bible to search for God's message to give me direction. I grew to appreciate the numerous challenges faced by the biblical characters and how they put their faith in God to sustain them—even when things didn't go well. And most importantly, I discovered God's unequivocal promise of love for all mankind, including me.

In addition to my father's family being founding members of Victory Baptist Church, my mother's parents were also founding members of another Baptist congregation. This one was located in the small western North Carolina rural town of Almond, near the Tennessee state line. My maternal grandmother was a strong-willed, staunch Baptist, and although it was my grandfather and other men's labor that helped build the physical structure, my grandmother was the strength behind the movement to get the congregation started and keep it vibrant through the years.

During the Depression, my grandmother taught school in a one-room schoolhouse and raised five children. With her husband working in a West Virginia coal mine, the only job he could obtain, she was left to provide much for her children. Widowed in her mid-fifties, and with the children grown, she lived many years by herself in a house that had an outdoor bathroom. She was what I call a "bootstrap woman." When life was tough, which was often for her, she first looked toward the heavens and prayed. Then she bent over, "pulled herself up by her bootstraps" and pressed forward, putting action beneath those prayers.

My mother inherited this bootstrap attitude. She, the youngest of the five children, had just turned 17 and had just completed her junior year of high school when her father died. After she graduated high school, she wanted to go to nursing school in Asheville, a city two hours away, but there was no college fund or any other money sitting in a bank with her name on it. So she looked toward the heavens, said a prayer, and then bent over and pulled herself up by her bootstraps. She picked apples from a nearby apple tree, carried several bushels to the main road, and set up an apple stand. The money she made from selling those apples for several months enabled her to pay her tuition to nursing school.

I come from that tough bootstrap lineage. I haven't had to be as resourceful in life as my mother and grandmother, but when I have to buckle down and make something happen to improve my situation, I've found the emotional resources within myself to do so.

When I was in my early twenties, I was living in Asheville by myself in an apartment, working a dead end job as an office manager, and in a defunct relationship with what was another one of the "great loves" of my life. Like my mother, and her mother before her, when things looked bleakest, I looked toward the heavens and said a prayer. Then I bent over, picked myself up by my bootstraps, and moved east to the larger city of Charlotte, North Carolina, two and half hours away. I arrived without a job and knew only one person, my married sister, who lived there. Yet I persevered, and years later, realizing it was the best decision I've ever made, I still call Charlotte home.

This "bootstrap attitude" has served me well many times since, with prayer as its foundation. Through my teenage, young adult years, and beyond, I have never stopped praying during tough times. But those prayers, or "pleas" as I came to see them, sounded a lot like, "God, me again. I need your help. Please fix (fill in the blank with the latest problem)."

Where were the prayers in the off-season—when everything was going fine? It was not unusual for none to occur. Yes, I was a plea-praying Baptist, and only on an as-needed basis.

I faithfully attended church all my life, until my post high school days. Once out of high school, single, working full time, with many friends and busy social Friday and Saturday nights, I started attending the "Church of the Inner Springs" most Sunday mornings. That would be bed springs. Sundays were, quite literally, a day of rest. From time to time, I'd visit a church, be it the one I grew up in or a friend's church, but not often.

It took until I married at the age of thirty before I migrated back into regular attendance. My husband, Tom, was a Catholic by birth and he'd converted to a Baptist in high school. We wanted to find a church home and decided to broaden our scope to visit Methodist and Presbyterian churches as well. It took us two years after we married to discover and finally join the congregation at St. John's Baptist Church in Charlotte. The version of worship was not the baptism-by-fear I'd grown up with and the people and activities offered gave us the feeling we were in the right place.

Four years after becoming part of this church, our daughter was born. We enrolled her in the "Cradle Roll" and she, too, became a Baptist by birth. I've served on numerous committees, regularly attended Adult Sunday school classes, and dutifully pledged and paid tithes. I've enjoyed the minister's sermons, and when times were tough for me, I remained loyal to my plea-praying routine. Sure, I had developed unresolved and unspoken questions about God, the hereafter, and my spiritual self over the years, but in my mind, these questions had plenty of time to be answered. I had a busy life as a wife and mother, with a full time career in a demanding sales job. It would be a long time before I had to figure these things out, so I kept my questions suppressed.

When cancer struck just before I turned 45, I faced the aspect of meeting God before I was quite willing to do so. With the diagnosis I discovered I wanted to truly know this God my parents and grandparents had embraced in their lives; the God I, too, had been embracing, but only on the surface; only on a ritual level, due to my birthright. I wanted, needed, to embrace God in a different and deeper way. I needed something more profound, more personal, and more spiritual. I needed something that felt like a real relationship, not a one-sided, plea-praying arrangement and conversation.

In the initial stages of my cancer journey, I realized that in those years since I was baptized in those lifesaving waters, I hadn't really found peace with my spirit, or with my beliefs. At night, when I lay my head on my pillow and the fear swirled around and through me, I began to hear the voice of the ministers from my youth, asking, "Where will you be in eternity—heaven or hell?"

As a self-proclaimed "bootstrap girl," facing cancer treatment and the possibility of this being a death sentence, I couldn't answer with certainty which one it would be.

 *Psalm 90:12*
Teach us to realize how short our lives are. Then our hearts will become wise.

*"The question is not whether the things
that happen to you are chance things
or God's things because, of course,
they are both at once.
There is no chance thing through which
God cannot speak—
even the walk from the house to the garage
that you have walked ten thousand times before,
even the moments when you cannot believe
there is a God who speaks at all anywhere."*

Frederick Buechner

Chapter One

Cancer Doesn't Run in My Family

We're together at Sunset Beach, North Carolina in early November 2002—Tracey, Barbara, Laura, Epsy, and me. We've been friends for many years, but our lives have us living in different parts of the eastern seaboard: New Jersey, Florida, and North Carolina. To stay connected with each other, we've committed to having annual reunions and this Sunset Beach weekend is our fourth. The house we're staying in is located on the inland side of the island away from the beach. There are no water views, but it offers us a fantastic place to relax and enjoy each other's company.

The weather has cooperated in a near perfect way, providing us a beautiful sunshine-filled fall weekend. We ride bikes around the off-season's quiet roads, walk on the beach and sit on the house's spacious back porch. The favorite activity, of course, is the non-stop talking, just as we always do at these reunions.

We're all in our early forties now, in great health, and generally pleased with life. There are a few of the usual gripes: the job not quite what we dreamed of, the husband who works too much, the weight gain in places we don't want. We share and talk about an assortment of topics. Talk of health problems, while surely lurking in our futures, has tiptoed into our dialogue over the past few years, but not often. Beyond the normal aches and pains, there really isn't much to be concerned about or worthy of discussion.

Until this trip.

For some reason, on this trip, this year, with all the perfection of the weather, food, and camaraderie, the topic of mammograms comes up.

I nonchalantly divulge that I had one—four years ago. My girlfriends are mortified that I've put off this procedure and over the next few hours, they harp on my lack of having had one since. They mention it so often they start to turn into annoying friends. On our second day together, we're in Laura's car, returning from a home tour excursion on Bald Head Island. Barbara, who is sitting with me in the backseat, brings up the subject yet again.

"So, Carol, are you going to make a mammogram appointment as soon as you get home?" she prods.

I look at her with an *I can't believe you're bringing that up again* look and respond with a shrug and a roll of my eyes, coupled with a good-natured laugh to (hopefully) show my good sense of humor. "It's really not a big deal," I say. "Cancer doesn't run in my family!" The subject is dropped—or at least I think it is.

That evening we cook in at the house and enjoy cocktails and a delicious shrimp dinner. We laugh, play cards, and talk some more. Suddenly, there's something else new as talk of goal-setting ensues. Goal-setting? We've never done goal-setting before. Why are we becoming so driven now? Isn't it enough we just plan to reunite a year from now? One by one, my friends divulge the goals they plan to accomplish before our next visit together. Given my position in our circle, and going in order, I'll be the last to share. I listen as they divulge theirs and think about what mine will be. I'm thinking—*my goal will be to change jobs*—but when it's my turn, I don't even get a chance to speak.

"Carol," they all say, practically in unison, "you will get a mammogram." I move from leaning forward in my chair at the table to falling back into my seat, flopping my body into an *I can't believe you guys* posture.

"What? That's my goal?" I guess it is, as they all seem very resolved. Tracey will later tell me how during her run on the beach that morning, as her thoughts wandered, she had a strong sensation that she needed to find a way to get me to make a mammogram appointment. It was important for me; she just knew it.

We depart at the end of that beautiful, peaceful weekend, feeling blessed to have been together once again. We are to communicate progress on our goals via e-mail. Once home, since I'm in no hurry to complete mine, I delay my promise to make a mammogram appointment until after the Christmas holidays. Early January, I call a local radiology practice referred to me by my ob-gyn. There's not much of a backlog and I secure an appointment for the end of the next week.

Mammograms are not fun, nor are they awful, but in general, it's an uncomfortable procedure at best. You arrive, are called back to the dressing area, and then told to strip down to the waist in order to put on the non-stylish, off-blue-with-some-sort-of-nothing, light-weight cotton smock that opens to the front. And no need to waste energy by tying the garment closed as it must remain open for the procedure. The air conditioning pops on and shoots air down your back to cool you off, whether you need it or not. You are then to sit patiently in the tiny chair provided in the dressing room, while you await your escort to the examining room. It's optional to thumb through the provided magazines. In time, the technician, who will be with you for the entire process, retrieves you from the dressing room. Holding the cotton smock closed to keep it from flying open, you make the short walk down a hallway, politely asking each other how you are today.

Once in the room where the X-rays are taken, you're then asked to stand in front of a tall, cold and impersonal machine, and lean in. With me, there isn't much to work with. My breasts are small, which is one of the reasons I've resisted this process.

On this day, the technician pulls and prods my breast to get it on that cold flat machine and then she turns the vice machine's squeeze on. She walks away to stand behind a protective plexiglass wall, only to say, "Don't breathe." Actually, not breathing is the easy part. Who can breathe when a part of your body is being squeezed into a position it doesn't belong? After each X-ray is taken, my breast is repositioned to obtain a different view, and the vice machine's squeeze is repeated.

Several squeezes later, I hear the words I'm desperate to hear: "We're done." I inhale a huge breath of gratefulness. The technician instructs me to sit down in the available chair in the X-ray room and wait for the doctor's review to make sure they have all they need. A few minutes later, the technician returns and I'm cleared for takeoff. I'm escorted back to the dressing room and to my belongings. I rush the removal of the smock, put on my clothes, and return to work. I've accomplished my assigned goal. My duty, for my girlfriends' benefit, is done. Now they can all relax and stop harassing me.

Two days later the phone rings in my office.

A kind woman's voice on the other end of the phone identifies herself as being with the radiologist office I have recently visited. She asks if I can come back in for some more X-rays—today. Today? As in immediately? Something with my right breast didn't look right, she says. I gulp for air. She comforts me by adding, "Given that it's been so long since your last mammogram, the difference between what we're seeing in the current X-rays could just be due to enhanced technology." Small comfort, but I take what I can get.

I'm able to jostle some work assignments and I return to the radiology office in the late afternoon. The drive is a blur. I suppose I stop at red lights when they are red and drive the appropriate speed limit. I don't really know. It's an out of body experience as I begin feeling some dread that I try to tell myself is unnecessary.

Cancer doesn't run in my family.

I put on the blue smock again and wait for the technician to escort me to the squeezing area. I don't bother to pick up or even look at the magazine in the dressing room. I just sit there, feeling a mixture of concern and dread. To my surprise, they don't take me back to the same room. This time they take me to a room where I can lie back on a comfortable medical-type bed, and to my relief, they do an ultrasound. Great things those ultrasound machines; there's no pain. The worst of it is the coldness of the gook they squeeze out of a tube and apply on the area to be examined, but it's not bad at all.

A radiologist physician, not a technician, is in charge of this procedure. She guides the wand over the breast area they are concerned about and stares at the black and white pictures on the monitor's screen. She speaks comforting words focused toward the monitor, "Can't tell that it's anything." Then she adds, "There's something showing up on the lower middle part of your right breast, but it's probably nothing to worry about."

She berates me somewhat for delaying a mammogram for four years, and then informs me that "we'll watch this area with a follow-up visit in six months." I'll have the pleasure of returning in July to do another mammogram or an ultrasound to check the area. I'm given strict orders to not postpone this appointment. For some reason, she seems to think I'm one of those women who would do that.

The appointment is set for July 20th. I make a mental note that I should be able to remember that date since it will be two days before I turn 45. Too young to have to worry about anything, and besides, cancer doesn't run in my family, remember?

I go home and sit down in front of my computer to e-mail my girlfriends; the ones that unknown to me at the time, with that goal-setting weekend, have placed me on a path to early detection.

 Proverbs 12:15
The way of a foolish person seems right to him. But a wise person listens to advice.

*"It does not matter how many times
you get knocked down,
but how many times you get up."*

Vince Lombardi

Chapter Two

Diagnosis

When I started to compile the chapters for this book, I couldn't find journal entries about the day I was diagnosed—aka, the Diagnosis Chapter. Where were the details of finding the lump, the multiple appointments, biopsies, and the fateful morning when I received the call delivering the bad news? Never written it seems. How could that be? The diagnosis is referenced in numerous parts of my story, but the details of the actual event were nowhere to be found.

So I finally sit, first taking pen to paper and eventually typing words into my computer—details of that "lost chapter"—details of the day I'd just as soon forget. Even then it's difficult, and words don't come easy. I make excuses to find other things to do. Clean the house, call a friend; anything but write about this stage of my journey; this diagnosis that wasn't supposed to happen. Not supposed to happen to me.

***

It's late June, and my husband, Tom, daughter, Lindsay, and I are at the beach again—this time for a week with our good friends, Jeff and Betsy and their children Emily and Matt. We're renting a house on Oak Island, North Carolina and the setting has all the makings of a relaxed vacation—leisurely mornings, swimming, beach reading, naps, evening walks, and late-night dinners—yet for the entire seven-day stretch, I'm out of synch with myself; I have the feeling that I'm not doing what I'm supposed to be doing.

A little voice inside my head is screaming, "Get busy! You've got things to do in life and you aren't doing them!"

During this period, Tom and I are also struggling with some issues in our marriage and have been seeing a counselor back home. I'm working hard at my sales job, but not really happy with the environment since new management took over a few months prior. Yet here I am, on a much-needed vacation with the opportunity to relax a little, but I just can't.

I do play in the ocean, alternately floating atop the mellow waves and body surfing the active ones. And since I'm in the water a lot, I towel off frequently after being in the ocean and after the end of the day showers. Why is this important? Because, after toweling off multiple times daily for a week, once the vacation is over and we return to our homes on Saturday, on Sunday evening, after taking a shower, I begin to towel dry, just as I had done numerous times over the past week, but now something is different. This time something has changed and my journey—the one I'd rather not go on—begins.

As I towel off from this shower, I feel a lump in my right breast, where the mammogram had created concern in January. I'm certain the lump wasn't there yesterday. My thoughts reel at first. "What's this?" I say aloud as I rub again. It's about the size of a quarter. I've never had a lump of any kind before and it alarms me. I usually live my life with a positive, upbeat, "glass half full" kind of attitude. Rare is it that I believe bad things are due to happen to me. When things haven't gone my way, like a bad job or a not so happy marriage, there's always time and ways to rectify the situation.

But now, as I stand in front of my bathroom mirror contemplating this lump, I feel a dark dread begin to take up residence in my spirit.

I dress and go into the living room where Tom is sitting on the sofa with his eyes closed. He isn't asleep. His eyes are burning as he's just put a dose of eye drops in and he's waiting for the drops to give him some relief. I sit down next to him and using a voice that doesn't even sound like my own, I say, "I have a lump on my breast."

He doesn't open his eyes, fatigued from his day of catching up on yard work. He responds nonchalantly, "It's probably nothing." Then he changes the subject to something completely unrelated. Something about a friend and whether we should get in touch with them to see how they're doing. Huh? Where is this coming from? My half-full glass is turning completely upside down and everything in it is pouring out. The Grim Reaper is hovering close and I'm worried. My husband isn't going to be my anchor—he's not even listening. What to do?

I get up off the sofa and head toward my bedroom, leaving him to rest his burning eyes. I lay down on the bed as tears start to escape down my cheek. I feel alone, very alone. What, or who do I turn to?

"God," I whisper into the emptiness of the room, "are you there? I think I might need you."

With my plea-praying in place, but also believing there are things we mere mortals must do to assist God with His work, my bootstrap demeanor kicks in. First thing Monday morning, I call the radiology clinic I'm scheduled to visit in three weeks for that follow-up mammogram. Unfortunately, they can't adjust their schedule enough to move my appointment up any sooner so I call my ob-gyn's office and explain about finding the lump. I ask if they can make a telephone call and try to get me an earlier appointment. They do a little better, but it's still more than a week away. Nine days. A long, hideous nine days of waiting.

The July 4th weekend is approaching and the backyard party we host each year for about 50 people is scheduled to go on as planned. My husband and I busy ourselves with the preparations. We have ribs and chicken cooked to perfection on the grill, and an assortment of other foods that provide our guests a fine feast. Several of our visiting friends ask what should be a simple, routine question, but one that challenges me throughout the day. "How are you?" they ask, and I give them the expected answer, hoping

I'm not lying when I respond, "I'm fine, thanks."

One of the couples visiting us for the party is our close friends, Jack and Deb. Since they live out of town, they're staying overnight. The day after the party, Deb and I are alone in the kitchen drinking tea while our husbands are outside. Deb senses something is bothering me, and asks.

I take one of the deep breaths that seem to be a normal thing for me to do lately, and tell her about the new addition to my body. She is genuine with her concern, and as it turns out, has an inside perspective of what I'm dealing with. She has experienced lumps herself on more than one occasion over the last several years. None have turned out to be cancerous, but it's always an emotional roller coaster ride until the diagnosis is confirmed, she says. Talking to her helps. It's the first real conversation where I've divulged my fears, and I'm grateful to confide in an understanding friend.

Finally, the day to have the follow-up mammogram arrives. I decide to go alone, accompanied only by my bootstrap attitude, convinced that everything is going to be fine.

When my name is called, I'm once again escorted back to the dressing room where I quickly change into the blue smock. I don't even glance at the magazines as I wait for the X-ray technician to retrieve me. I'm anxious to get going, so I stand, not even sitting down in the tiny chair, ready to come out through the door of this small room like a rodeo bull waiting on the gates to open so it can get into the ring. When the knock on the door comes, I'm ready.

"Lead the way," I say, as I'm escorted to another ultrasound. The radiologist rolls the ultrasound's wand over my breast and says to the monitor's screen, "I'm not sure about the lump, but what is that?" Now turning and talking to me instead of the screen, she explains that there's something else showing up toward my armpit. She suggests a biopsy, and soon. However, due to scheduling, they don't have time to do the biopsy at that moment, but "if I could just thumb through some magazines in the waiting room, they can do that procedure in about three hours."

I find it hard to breathe, but hear myself say that I'd be glad to wait the three hours for us to get this done and over with today. I change back into my normal clothing to make myself presentable in the public waiting room and find a chair in a people-watching corner. Patients come and go and I pretend to be interested in articles on women's health—something I'm wondering if I've failed at.

I'm the only person left in the waiting room when they finally call my name and escort me back. Using a small needle, and an ultrasound as a guide, they pull samples of various areas out of my breast. When they're done, I'm told to keep an ice pack on the site for a short while, to not to do any heavy lifting, and that they'll call me in a few days with the results. It's Wednesday. I go through my normal work and home routines, all the while trying not to worry, and on Friday morning at 10:00 a.m., the phone in my office rings.

How does one intuitively know that their life is about to change? While I rarely close the door to my office, instinctively, before answering the phone, I reach out and shut it. I pick up the receiver, and with a slight hesitation in my voice, I say, "Hello, this is Carol" to the radiologist on the other end of the line.

There's a brief dialogue that I don't recall, other than she informs me she's phoning from out of town. Then I hear the three words that I've been dreading: "You have cancer."

My grip on the phone's receiver tightens as I try to listen. The lump is benign, she explains, but the cancer is in the upper area of my breast—toward my armpit. The doctor then tells me I'll need a surgeon and she gives me a couple of names to call.

I hang up the phone and somehow manage to keep my composure as I sit for a moment or two, dumbfounded. I stare wide-eyed in disbelief at the phone wondering, how can this be? Then I call Tom.

When he answers, I don't say hello; he'll just have to recognize my quivering voice as I blurt out, "The doctor just called and I have breast cancer!" He's supportive, and he offers words of encouragement. "We'll handle this, Carol," he says. I'm sure he's thinking, as I am, *not sure how*, but his words calm me, temporarily.

The next telephone call seems more difficult than telling my husband—telling my parents. They know I'm waiting on the test results, and when I say hello to my mom, she's quick to ask, "Everything turn out okay?"

With my breath feeling like it's just been knocked out of me, I push through the smothering feeling and somehow manage to get my voice to answer. "No, Mom," I say, "it's cancer." I'll never forget her "Oh" response as long as I live. I don't remember much else about the conversation other than my dad getting on their second phone for the three of us to talk together. The conversation ends with them telling me, "We love you" and those three words do much to offset the anguish of the three-worded diagnosis I've just received.

The next person I call from that bad news telephone is my boss, Vern. He's in his office just across the hall from mine and by this time, the tears are threatening.

"Vern, can you come into my office, please?" I ask. He must have heard the anxiety in my voice, as he arrives and knocks on my office door within seconds.

He comes in, closes the door, and sits down in a chair across from me. With little success at holding back my tears, I tell him my news. He gives me his full support in whatever needs to be done. Then he says, "Carol, I think we need to pray about this. Would that be okay?" Even though I know Vern is a Christian, his offer is still a pleasant surprise and I realize it's exactly what I need.

I nod my head up and down to answer since the words, "yes, please" seem stuck in my throat. He reaches out and takes hold of both of my hands, which is something we don't do in our business sales office—and he prays. Vern lifts my family and me up to God, asking for His presence in mine, Tom's and Lindsay's lives; to strengthen us as we deal with cancer. It's a powerful prayer, one I wish I've recorded, as I sense it will come in handy in the coming days. Instead, I can only try to remember how his prayer makes me feel, surrounded by the love and support of a friend, and a higher power.

The rest of the day is a numb blur. There's a conference call I have to be on, and I sit there listening to the dialogue, but absorbing nothing. I'm in my own stressed world, beginning a game with the "head monsters" who are wanting me to come out and play. Somehow I manage to work the remainder of the day, then head home to try and figure things out.

It's only three little words—"You have cancer"—but I sense those three little words are about to change my life and set me, my family, and friends who love me, on an arduous journey to I don't know where.

 Psalm 23:4
Even though I walk through the darkest valley, I will not be afraid.
You are with me. Your shepherd's rod and staff comfort me.

Courage

Carol Fore Injaychock

You are so very courageous.
Am I?
Well, yes. I know I couldn't face all that you are facing.
And look at you; you look great!
Thank you.
She courageously smiles at her friend and her naive
compliment.

Courageous?

The lion traveled through Oz
Looking for his courage.
She travels through a Cancer Maze
Looking for hers.

Courageous?

What then is this sick feeling in the pit of her stomach--fear?
Why won't the head monsters quiet down--fear?
Why does she sit and stare
At nothing at all
Wide-eyed
With her thoughts toward heaven,
Pondering if she'll have her questions answered about that
place sooner than she'd like?
Fear?

Courageous?

Is facing something because you
have to
Courage?

Does she possess the traits of Courage?
Bravery
Valor
Daring
Heroism

She ponders Webster's definition, "Ability to conquer fears or despair."

Courageous?

Not yet.
Not
quite
yet.

Like the lion, she cries often;
Rocks back and forth with fear.

Each day,
each and every day,
she faces the foe.

Each and every day,
She does what she must do.
She visits her doctors,
Continues her treatments.

She faces her immortality.
She consults with an attorney and initiates a Will.
She purges her possessions, so her survivors won't have to.
She holds many of her friends' hands, and comforts them.

She
   Prays.
     Hopes.
       Loves.

          Lets Go.
          Lets God.

Courageous?

    Yes,
       she
         is.

"Sometimes you put walls up
not to keep people out,
but to see who cares enough
to break them down."

Anonymous

Chapter Three

Letting Others In

I ready for my cancer fight like a matador entering a bullring. I am facing the largest bull I could ever possibly imagine confronting and its snarling puffing nostrils, angry eyes, and sharp horns are pointed squarely in my direction. All I seem to have is an itsy bitsy red cape that I'm supposed to wave in his direction. I feel alone, like I'm standing in the middle of thousands of empty stadium seats, facing this ferocious beast. I'm in disbelief. How can I possibly win?

I know I need a few people in those seats; a few people in my corner to cheer me on. But telling them, allowing them in, is hard. Asking for their help is harder.

Our only child, Lindsay, has just turned nine and her birthday celebration with several of her friends, which has been scheduled for a while, will go on as planned the day after my diagnosis. It's heart-wrenching to think about what our eventual conversation will be like. How can I protect her and keep her in the safe and secure world I want her to live in? What will the word "cancer" mean to her? This isn't something I should have to tell her. Not now. Not ever.

The party provides a welcome diversion to my fears. The eight girls there to celebrate with Lindsay bust the piñata and scramble for the candy, play games, eat birthday cake and ice cream, and enjoy their time with each other. We aren't sure when we'll tell her but decide it won't be this day. This day belongs to her. We tuck her into bed that evening and let her smile at the memories of being surrounded by friends and gifts of love. The bad news can wait. She deserves this happiness.

The next morning, we eat breakfast and dress for church. Tom and I have no immediate intent of telling her this morning either—we're still unsure whether we'll even share the news this day. But once at church, and sitting in my Sunday school classroom surrounded by friends I have known for 12 years, I can feel myself starting to break down. At the end of the lesson time, when we typically swap cares and concerns, I open my mouth to share my news. I want to be composed, but I'm struggling to speak. I sit up straighter in an effort to gain strength, inhale, grip the side of my chair, and just blurt it all out.

"I've got news," I start, "and it isn't good. I have breast cancer, and in a few weeks, I'm probably going to be having some sort of surgery."

I look around the room at the fear registering on their faces. Once I've finished, I receive plenty of hugs and sincere concern and I feel their loving support. I reel in my emotions to leave the classroom and attend worship services in the sanctuary where apparently, my news spreads like wildfire, because as soon as worship service ends, a woman comes up to Tom, and with Lindsay standing right beside him, says, "I'm so sorry about Carol." Lindsay's eyes grow wide as she looks up at her dad and asks, "What's wrong with Mommy?"

There's no avoiding the conversation now. Back at home, sitting around the dining room table, Tom and I tell Lindsay that I have cancer in my breast. Maybe the meltdown at church has served its purpose, as I'm calm and composed with her—my most important audience. We tell her that we don't know what will happen, that I'll be going to many doctors, that I'll probably need some surgery, and that I'll be fine.

"But you don't even look sick," she says.

My not looking sick and our calm demeanor seem to give her comfort; she reacts to the news well and doesn't become upset.

Besides my parents and my Sunday school classmates, initially,

I decide to keep most of the other stadium seats empty. Save for the doctors and nurses who are mandated to be in my corner, I'm a bootstrap matador, and vow to fight the fight with the least amount of drama and inconvenience to others as possible.

Which works for a while, but I quickly find, not really what I need going forward.

While telling others is hard, bit by bit I start to reach out and invite friends, other family members, and acquaintances into the bullring with me. This is not an easy thing for a self-sustaining, bootstrap woman, but I need support. I need help.

I need a good surgeon.

I already have a few names, but I'm thinking I could use some more. Immediately after the diagnosis, being unfamiliar with the medical world, I had contacted a doctor friend I know. Okay, so he delivers babies and doesn't treat breast cancer, but it's a start. Doctors tend to know other doctors due to professional proximity, and this doctor friend tells me about someone he knows. The radiologist who delivered my diagnosis gave me some recommendations too. And it seems that God, my higher power, was also going to swoop in and bring me friends and serendipitous events to assist with my decision.

The afternoon of Lindsay's birthday party, parents of one of the girls, Mitch and Katie, who are good friends of ours, had been invited to spend the post-party afternoon with us and visit by the pool. I wasn't sure I would still be up for an extended visit due to the previous day's diagnosis, but rather than reschedule, Tom and I had decided to act as "normal" as possible and just try to enjoy an afternoon with old friends.

Looking through my kitchen window and watching our friends as they walked up our driveway, I knew they were in a frame of mind to have a leisurely, relaxing afternoon, sitting by our pool, catching up. I remember thinking, "Dare I? Tell them?" They didn't ask to take a seat in my bullring. They didn't even know there was a fight brewing.

I gave them time to settle in and relax a little. I felt certain my anxiety was showing, but they didn't seem to notice. After about 30 minutes, my husband and Mitch walked over to the horseshoe pit, out of earshot of Katie and me. Katie then asked me that polite, usually non-interesting question, "So, how are you?" It had been months, which felt like years, since we'd last visited with each other. To thank them for coming, I took a deep breath and said, "Well, you see, Katie, I had this lump, which is right here" pointing unashamedly to my lower right breast, "and I had a biopsy done, and, well, it was benign."

Her eyes grew wide, then seemed to show relief, then grew wide again when I added, "But ....."

" ....they did an ultrasound and found something tucked under my arm, and they did a biopsy of that, and well, Friday, yesterday, they called and, well, uh," as Katie reached out to grab my hand, for she knew the words were struggling to come out, "I have breast cancer, Katie, and I don't know what to do!"

Her eyes settled back into her sockets and she held my hand and said several endearing things, which included, "Oh, Carol. I'm so very sorry." Then she put on her angel wings and asked, "Do you remember meeting Denise?"

I nodded my head up and down like a lost puppy, to indicate that I did remember her friend. Katie reminded me that Denise worked for a "wonderful oncologist," named Dr. White. She said that Dr. White had the reputation for being one of the very best cancer doctors and surgeons in Charlotte, or elsewhere for that matter.

"Do you think Denise would help me get in touch with him?" I asked. This asking for help thing was new for me and I was uncomfortable with the notion. Yet, unbeknownst to both of us, Katie had helped me start down that road of "letting others in." Holding tight to my hand that day, Katie had helped me start filling the empty seats in my bullring with many loving angels.

Fast forward a few days and today I run Katie's recommendation by my radiologist. She agrees that it's a good choice, but is curious why I have chosen him. It seems silly to tell her, "because he showed up on my doorstep and jumped into my lap!" so aloud I answer, "A friend knows him" and the radiologist makes an appointment for me.

Now, with barely a week having passed since my conversation with Katie, I'm sitting in Dr. White's waiting room with my husband. From there we're escorted to a medical exam room where we sit some more, waiting for the doctor's arrival. Soon there's a knock on the door, and without a moment's delay, the door opens and standing there in her white smock and Type A, excited-about-life personality, is Denise.

"You will love Dr. White," she says. "And whatever you need from me, you just let me know. I can help you through the medical maze."

This stranger, this angel, takes a seat in my bullring of her own accord. It's a good lesson to learn. Some people wait to be asked. Others jump in on their own. Seems most just want to be invited.

I know I need to use their energy when I don't have enough of my own. To not try to go it alone. To fill the seats in my bullring with as many human angels as possible. I am starting to believe that this supportive love from friends, family, and even strangers can help me fight the ferocious beast and together, we can win.

"Ole!"

 Ecclesiastes 4:9-10
Two people are better than one. They can help each other in everything they do. Suppose someone falls down. Then his friend can help him up. But suppose the man who falls down doesn't have anyone to help him up. Then feel sorry for him!

"Nobody who ever gave his best regretted it."

George Halas

Chapter Four

Life is Like a Ten-Speed Bicycle

Dr. White has performed two surgeries on me in seven-weeks' time. Today I'm lying on my sofa recuperating from the second surgery when my friend Betsy calls. I hear the dread in her voice and I'm concerned. Obviously upset, she tells me that our mutual friend, Tim, has died. He was only 49 years old. He'd gone hiking, she says, as he often did, on a Blue Ridge Parkway trail close to his home. When he hadn't returned by dark, his concerned wife contacted authorities, who then searched the area and found him dead of a heart attack on the trail.

The first time I met Tim, ten years ago, I immediately liked him. He'd recently been hired to the sales team I worked with. On his first day on the job, he walked into the office, and I was standing in the foyer; the first to greet him. I stuck out my hand to introduce myself. Within seconds, his positive energy energized me. He had a gleam in his eye, a peppy gait when he walked, the talent to tell an appropriate joke at the appropriate time, and an ability to recite word for word almost any Andy & Barney dialogue from The Andy Griffith Show. When Tim was around, laughter followed.

We worked together for several years and he became a friend who brightened many days by his mere presence or by just hearing his voice on the phone. He loved his wife, Karen, his dog, Amos, and the great outdoors. I knew him to be active and fit; regularly biking on his 10-speed, running, hiking, rappelling, camping, and traveling. He embraced life with enthusiasm and made life better for those of us who were lucky to know him.

I changed jobs after several years of working with him, but when we could, we talked on the phone and saw each other from time to time. When he heard about my diagnosis, he called immediately and we talked briefly. But even Tim couldn't find much to laugh about in my situation. The subject of cancer can suck the joy right out of any conversation, even one with someone as optimistic as Tim. Over the past couple of months, we'd continued to communicate by e-mail and just a couple of days ago, on the evening prior to this second surgery, he'd sent me an encouraging e-mail, saying, "I'm praying that the 'Big Guy' will take care of you. Fight the fight, Carol. Prayers are being sent your way."

Now Betsy is telling me he's gone?

I can't speak; I'm in shock. I still have his e-mail in my computer's in-box. He was alive two days ago! And now he's gone? And why now? Not Now! Please not now! We still need him. *I* still need him. I need his laughter now more than ever. How can this be? What is God thinking? What is God doing?

I have a tube coming out of my armpit from surgery and I'm weak, but against my body's better judgment, I go to Tim's funeral; a two and a half hours drive time away. My friends—Steve, Betsy and Bobby—help me. Steve drives and Betsy sits in the backseat with me and my pillow to help keep me comfortable. It's a dreary September day with a misty rain. Even if the sun manages to shine on us, this day will still be dreary and painfully, painfully sad.

We sit in a large church's full sanctuary and say good-bye. It's obvious that Tim has developed plenty of work relationships throughout his career. Many of those people are here to honor him today. But none of his work awards nor any of the sales goals he achieved are mentioned. Not once. I listen as several friends tell memorable stories of Tim's adventures with life, of which there are plenty. At the end of the service, the minister sums it up best by saying, "If life is like a ten-speed bicycle, Tim lived with all of his gears engaged." He had indeed been engaged with all the gears of life, complete with a positive attitude where he embraced and actively participated in all that he could.

Tim's life was cut short much too soon. It's ironic that in the same newspaper that announces his unexpected death, there's an article about a guy that jumped off a bridge in Tim's hometown and committed suicide. When I read this, I scream to God, "You had a volunteer! If you needed another angel, you had someone else. Why take Tim?"

Tim said he'd be praying for me. He has a direct line to the "Big Guy" now, so not wanting to bother God too much, I reach out to Tim and ask him to tell God that I really would like to stay here a while longer—at least to see my daughter grown. I know he'll do what he can, possibly with a joke inserted somewhere within the request, but with the appropriate sentiment to get the job done.

 1 Corinthians 9:24

In a race all the runners run. But only one gets the prize. You know that, don't you? So run in a way that will get you the prize.

*"The stories of past courage can offer
hope and provide inspiration.
But they cannot supply courage itself.
For this, each man must look
into his own soul."*

John F. Kennedy

Chapter Five

Let Go and Let God

These days I go where my doctors tell me to go—get a mammogram, a MRI, a biopsy, a bone scan, a CT scan, and more scans, scans, scans. Everything, and I mean everything, is scanned several times over, and as I lie on the tables, close my eyes and listen to the roar of the machines, words and phrases begin to appear in my brain and imprint themselves on my psyche:

Let Go and Let God.

Let Go and Let God.

Let Go and Let God.

This mantra helps to shut down those other voices inside my head. The ones that sound like:

What if they find more?

Am I going to die?

Why me?

How sick will chemo make me?

What will these doctors make me do next?

I wonder how long that lady in the obituary lasted after she was diagnosed?

The constant scans and doctor visits are daunting. It feels like I've been thrown into a maze of narrow dark passages that meander into oblivion. I do have the benefit of directions given to me by appropriate medical authorities, telling me which way to turn and when to do it. Walking down those passages, however, leaves me angry, confused, scared, and depressed. In the darkness of my spirit, I reach out to my higher power, close my eyes, inhale, and pray my admittance:

"God, I don't think I can do this."

Then with a plea for help, I ask, "Can I turn this over to you? Will you help me find a peace that will enable me to make it through whatever I need to do?"

My plea-praying is beginning to feel more like an alliance with God, instead of the fix-all solo performance I'm used to asking of Him. I wonder if he notices the difference and is proud of my progress.

Yet I'm disappointed that I'm not given a burning bush like Moses; a visual sign that my prayers are actually being heard. But what I do get is an intuitive peace that feels as though it comes from above, telling me, "I am here." Much like Moses as he faced God's presence on the mountain, I believe God hears my cry from the cancer wilderness; I believe he sees my misery and is concerned for my suffering. God guided Moses and I believe He will guide me, too.

Is everything suddenly better? No. Not always. In the days that follow, the stress of dealing with cancer often threatens to dominate the peace. However, running parallel is the knowledge that God is always there—in the wings. I often have to quiet myself and my thoughts, inhale, exhale, pray, and let Him take over and in the moments I do manage to let go, I get what I need—peace, if only for a moment.

Cancer is bigger than me, and I need someone, something, bigger than cancer to help me fight it. I need someone who can light up my world with the light of peace.

I call that someone, God.

 Matthew 11:28
Come to me, all you who are tired and carry heavy loads. I will give you rest.

"You never know how strong you are until being strong is the only choice you have."

Unknown

Chapter Six

Crystal Balls

I have to admit that I've struggled most of my life with the wise counsel to live in the moment, especially when uncertainty is looming. I have a long history of looking for the proverbial crystal ball. I want to see my future so I know with certainty that I'm making the right decision and that everything will turn out for the better.

Now my desire to know my future is intensified. I look for the crystal ball to show me my future in everything. Even in my prayers. "Please God," I find myself pleading, "give me a sign that I'm going to be okay." Then I get specific: "Please provide me a white dove." An obvious religious sign is required, don't you think? Instead, what I get is a pigeon walking around my driveway.

"Close enough, God, thanks," I say, thanking God for the acknowledgement, however small.

I look for signs in what friends and even complete strangers say to me. "I'm sure you'll be okay." Good to know, since the person telling me this is obviously of keen intelligence, although without his or her own crystal ball as far as I can tell. I try to convince myself if he or she thought so, it must be a good sign. I plead for my doctors to tell me my future, too. "Tell me, will I get really sick? Will I lose my hair? Will my cancer come back?"

Oh, how I want to believe that I will be an anomaly and surprise all of my educated, experienced doctors, and manage to keep my hair. Although I hold on to this fantasy with weak faith, I resist the full acceptance that it's going to happen for real, to me.

And being a planner, as well as a worrier, just in case I do lose my hair, I need to know what I am embarking on and how best to survive.

A cancer survivor, who I meet through a friend, tells me about an upcoming seminar sponsored by the American Cancer Society called "Look Good, Feel Better." It's being held at the Cancer Center of my local hospital. When I enter the room, I've had two surgeries behind me and am two days away from beginning chemo. I look good. I feel good. To anyone glancing in my direction, I give no outward appearance of having a cell-busting beast inside my body.

I take my seat and survey the 12 ladies sitting in the room with me. Most of them seem to be in the midst of their treatments and are wearing scarves or wigs on their heads. One woman has her bald head displayed, seemingly oblivious to thinking there should be anything to hide. Will that be me? Is that my future?

I stare wide-eyed and force myself to smile. Do I look scared? Desperate? I hope not, but fear forms inside and ties me up in emotional knots. I survey their faces and decide they all look tired. "It's 7:00 p.m. It's been a long day," I tell myself. "Of course they look tired."

Then our seminar leader, a beauty consultant, wants to have a headscarf tying demonstration. She asks everyone wearing a wig to remove it. Off come ALL the wigs. Wait, this blonde sitting beside me is bald? That was a wig? It's amazing how real it looked! I gaze into the now available multiple crystal balls with much discomfort as I receive my futuristic reading.

Let's face it. I'm screwed.

Miss Beauty Consultant shows us how to best wrap and secure a scarf around our heads and suggests looking for one with a soft cotton texture, much like a t-shirt. "Your head's skin is tender, and softer material will feel better," she explains. Around the room, we all struggle to tie our scarves into proper position. Feeling like an imposter, I notice the process works better on the bald heads than it does for me with my still abundant and protruding locks.

The fun part (this part really is "fun," if you can put the word "fun" in a cancer journey) is the makeover, which starts out much like other make-up parties I've attended before. I get to pick out the colors that best fit my skin tone from numerous offerings of blush, eye makeup, and foundation. It's all there. But now I'm learning how to pencil in eyebrows that will no longer be around; how to enhance my eyes when my eyelashes are gone.

I look around the room at these women, and I "see" my future in all of those bald heads and those tired eyes and I'm not sure I like it.

At the end of the seminar I'm a bit rattled, but prepared. Well, I think I'm prepared anyway. As I leave, I smile and say thank you and even hug some of the attendees, offering my well wishes as we chatter on about how nice this evening has been. I leave holding my gift bag, thinking I have hit the make-up jackpot, a small consolation prize for my emotions which are going places I don't want them to go. And when I get home, all I want is to be alone, with my full head of hair, eyebrows, and eyelashes.

I go to our bathroom to take a shower. Here I can cry my private tears. Everything is becoming too much, too real, and to God and the showerhead I plead, "Please tell me I'll be okay. Can you, please?"

I close my eyes and as the water rushes down and over my distressed spirit, I sense God's calming presence and relax, ever so slightly, if only for a moment.

 Psalm 91:4
He will cover you with his wings. Under the feathers of his wings, you will find safety. He is faithful. He will keep you safe like a shield or tower.

"We must be willing to let go of the life we planned so as to have the life that is waiting for us."

Joseph Campbell

Chapter Seven

Most Survive

"Most survive breast cancer. There's no reason why you shouldn't be one of them."

These are the first words out of my primary oncologist's mouth at our initial consultation. As I stand in his office, I don't realize I'm not breathing until I hear these words. Then I exhale so hard, I almost fall backwards. He's just delivered the human encouragement I need to keep going.

Lately it seems I've been focusing on the negative and am in dire need of an attitude adjustment.

I've always known that regardless of what we battle in life—illness, divorce, loss of job, or death of a loved one—most can, and will, survive the crisis. And while some of us may have very difficult circumstances and journeys, how we navigate the process depends, in large part, on our attitude.

If you're like me, during a crisis, I need an extra amount of tender loving care and assistance. Often this comes through friends, counseling, and if need be, medication. To survive is good. And to survive with hope for a better life is the foundation of an optimistic attitude. But with all the negative information out there, sometimes it's hard to get to that positive place, and even harder to stay there.

Since I've started this journey, I've tried to stay away from statistics—you know, the percentage of women my age, with my type of cancer, who have (or haven't) survived after five, ten, fifteen years? A friend, and breast cancer survivor, warned me early on, "You can make yourself crazy and paranoid with all the information available on the internet."

I've tried to ignore the numbers and diagrams and "horror stories." I've looked to my doctors to give me the information I need and medically speaking, I feel I know what I need to know: I have breast cancer. It's just shy of Stage 3. I'm at high risk for it coming back, and I'm fighting the hideous beast with surgery, chemo and radiation.

I thought I had built a resistant wall against negativity, but didn't realize that cracks were forming. While I thought I was filling my head with positive energy and information, I didn't realize how much I needed that validation until I heard my doctor's words.

From this moment on, I vow to do my utmost to focus on optimism. If 10 percent survive, I can be that ten. If my risk of recurrence is 80 percent, I can be in the other twenty. I can, I can, I can feed my mind positive thoughts and positive outcomes can follow.

Am I burying my head in the sand? Maybe.

I begin to embrace the realization of death being a part of our natural lives; after all, 100 percent of us will die one day; we don't know when, but it will happen. I just don't want to get there anytime soon.

Up until now, I've lived my life as though tomorrow would come, and keep coming. I have time and plenty of it. Time to fix whatever doubts I have about God and the afterlife. Time to fix the relationships that have been damaged. Time to travel. Time to work. I'm young. The world is awaiting me.

My cancer diagnosis is bringing me face to face with the reality of death. It's forcing me to realize that it can happen to me; that life and all my well-deserved time on this earth, can be taken away, at any moment. This is a very rude, but necessary, enlightenment. I've been guilty, as most of us are, of taking life for granted.

So I step toward chemo with the knowledge that I can do this. That I can survive. And not just barely. I can survive with hope in the knowledge that each day is a gift and a day to accomplish the things God has intended for me.

 John 14:27
I leave my peace with you. I give my peace to you. I do not give it to you as the world does. Do not let your hearts be troubled. And do not be afraid.

"Peace comes within. Do not seek it without."

Buddha

Chapter Eight

Welcome to The Drip Lounge

Welcome to my cancer party, held in "The Drip Lounge" every other Thursday at one o'clock.

My friend, Maria, a cancer survivor, coined this phrase; an apt description for the room that awaits me; the room filled with faux-leather recliners, medicine poles, and infusion bags. But before I'm lucky enough to step inside, I'm to meet with Dr. Frenette who will walk me through the chemo stage of this journey.

Tom and I sit in yet another waiting room. This one is filled with numerous chairs; some filled with people and some empty and I have to wonder—do they really need this many chairs on any given day? Seriously? Are there that many of us?

A few of the women waiting here wear wigs and a few wear bandanas or scarves. Some wear ball caps. One of the women and a couple of the men allow their bald heads to bear witness to the struggle. None of them look scared; most just seem resolved to forge ahead. I make brief eye contact with one bald-headed woman and then quickly look away—embarrassed that she'll see in my face and eyes, my fear for her, my fear for me.

A nurse in a blue smock comes to the door and calls out my name. Like so many others before me, I rise, prepared to leave my "normal life" behind. Do I really have to do this? The note on the reception area reads, "If your wait lasts more than 30 minutes, please notify receptionist." It's okay, really. I can sit out here all day and be just fine. No rush. Take your time.

Unlike so many doctor visits where I really do wish they'd

hurry up, this waiting room visit is actually too short-lived. As I walk down the hall, I mentally hold on to the encouragement given to me earlier in the day via a phone conversation with Anne, another survivor mentor, who told me, "Don't worry. You won't glow or anything after you're done."

"How are you today?" the blue smock asks politely.

"Fine, and I hope you are." The pleasantry comes out of my mouth like a well-rehearsed speech. What I really want to say is, "I'm fine! I'm fine! I'm alive, and alive is fine! Having hair is fine! Facing chemo, well, that's not so fine!" but I just smile and keep on walking. She escorts us past a nurse's station where rows of medical files are stored, readily accessible, should one of the patients whose lives are held in the treatment's hands need to be updated with the latest change, development, or God forbid, complication.

Tom and I are motioned into a small room. I sit down in a black, inflexible, and somewhat comfortable chair. There is also a high, off the floor, patient lounging chair with its luxurious tissue paper sheet in ready position. The glistening chrome medicine cabinets look to be freshly polished. The blue linoleum floors, with their splatters of whites and swirls of mauve, are pristine clean. It is all very sterile. I think unimportant thoughts about how the medical community could use an interior decorator. The blue smock takes my temperature and blood pressure. She tells us, "The doctor will be here soon" and quietly exits the room, closing the door behind her. The quiet hangs over Tom and me as I stare down at the linoleum, in no mood to think anymore, or to decorate.

There's a knock on the door and my heart goes to my throat. For just a moment, I look around the room for a place to hide. What would be even better is if Scotty, from Star Trek, could beam me up right about now. But I answer the knock with a flat-toned, "Come in" and wonder what the doctor would do if I instead said, "Stay away."

Wide-eyed, with a forced smile on my lips, I look at Dr.

Frenette, who truly is a wonderful doctor. When you put your life in someone's hands, you should consider them to be wonderful, don't you think? He sits down in a chair across from us and gives the helpful blah blah blah conversation about what to expect.

"Blah blah blah, lose hair in about two weeks, blah blah blah call if anything occurs that you're uncertain about, blah blah blah take medicine, blah blah blah."

I look down at the blue linoleum and shuffle my feet. He keeps talking. Once he pauses and I look up and ask, "Are you sure? Are you positive I'll lose my hair?"

He's heard this before, I'm sure, and with kind, sympathetic, matter-of-fact eyes, he answers, "Yes, two weeks from this first treatment."

I look away, feeling defeat. Staring down again, I make one last, desperate attempt. "Are you certain?"

"Yes," he repeats and continues with his blah blah blahs.

"How will I react to the treatments?" I hear my voice asking. "Will I get sick?"

"You'll have to tell me," he answers. "Everyone's different. I'll treat you as the individual you are and we'll figure this out as we move through the process."

I'm lost to myself and this new world I've entered. I so want him to change his mind about the hair, but sensible enough to know that it is what it is, and I move on. "Will I lose weight?"

"Probably not. Most people gain weight due to the hunger sensations the treatments produce."

I inhale, and while so many sarcastic comments come to mind, I let them go. "What are my physical limitations?" I ask instead.

"Do what you feel like doing."

He continues with his instructions, which includes that if we drink alcoholic beverages, to not drink more than one glass of wine. And then, only occasionally. I enjoy a good glass of wine on occasion, but adding alcohol to the harsh chemicals that will be going into my system doesn't seem like such a great idea.

There are probably more questions to ask. I just don't know

what they are.

The blue smock reappears and escorts us back to the waiting room. After a few minutes, a new nurse calls my name and again, Tom and I rise from our chairs. I put one foot in front of the other and walk forward. Slowly, but forward. We follow the lead of this sweet new nurse with her multi-colored smock to a large room that is clearly bustling, and crowded.

We enter through a door labeled "Infusion Area." The room is very open, with windows lining the entire long wall that faces me, letting in sunlight to temporarily brighten this dreary moment. I'm nervous. There are about 30 recliner chairs lined up around the walls and most are already occupied with people receiving treatments. The temperature is cool, or did my blood just evaporate? The pinging noises of the multiple machines are methodically making their presence known. Like Morse code to my ears, saying, "I am here. I make you well."

"Where would you like to sit?" the nurse asks.

I'm thinking, in my car, with my seat belt snug and secure, getting the hell out of Dodge. Instead, I point straight ahead to one of the empty chairs. I look at my husband with questions in my eyes that neither he nor I are capable of answering. The nurse escorts me to the tan recliner where I'm to spend the next three hours. Tom sits to my right front, the nurse to my left. I manage to force a laugh a time or two at something I say, or the nurse says, in an effort to lighten the mood.

Since my lumpectomy surgery is on my right side, the needles and tubes for administering the treatments will go into my left. I'm told they put the treatments into your leg if you've had surgery on both sides, so a tiny victory there. I also have great veins that the nurse admires, and I'm thankful for this additional mercy, which means I don't have to have another procedure; a port installed under my skin.

Across the room is a lady who can't get her veins to cooperate. She'll have to reschedule. She'll return after she has her surgery to put the port in. How cruel. To have yourself in this room ready to go, having dreaded this day, only to be told it won't happen, all because a little vein isn't working right.

The nurse talks to me about the medicines they're going to give me to take home. These will be my anti-nausea arsenal. There's a timeframe, she explains, where they're most effective and I'm glad my husband is taking notes. Too much for my numb, scared brain to deal with.

"How was your morning sickness during pregnancy?" she asks. My eyes go wide with what I'm sure is a very confused look.

"None at all," I manage to respond.

"Well, that seems to be a good thing. Most of our female patients who've had minimal morning sickness often don't have much trouble with the nausea from chemo."

Another nurse brings a blanket over to cover my now chilled body. The blanket is warm like it just came out of a dryer. I snuggle in. There are offers of soda and crackers. I'm hooked up to the appropriate tubes and the medicines begin their drip into my veins, creating a cold ache up my arm which concerns me. First, the anti-nausea medicines, then the chemo Adriamycin, fondly referred to as the "Red Devil" (because it's bright red and a devil of a treatment), and another drug, Cytoxin. I pull the warmth of the blanket tighter around me.

I look at Tom and my eyes say, "Here we go. I'm scared. Thanks for being here." My head starts to feel a little dizzy, like I've just had very large glass of wine. There's a small TV available and magazines to read. I do neither. I talk to Tom, close my eyes and rest some, and contemplate this new life I've found myself in.

About three hours later, treatment number one of eight is finished and I'm told I can leave. I stand and walk unassisted to the restroom. I'm somewhat groggy and ready, SO VERY READY, to go home, but first, I need to pee.

The restroom is twice as large as a normal public restroom. I suppose it's made that way to accommodate either a wheel chair, an infusion stand, or a second person to be able to assist the patient. Then, "Oh my!" for I didn't expect the toilet to be full of red when I stood to flush. Wait, did I bleed? The toilet looks like a red punch bowl. No, it's just the "Red Devil." I roll my eyes. Unbelievable. That "Red Devil" will get you every time.

 Job 12:10

He holds the life of every creature in his hand. He controls the breath of every human being.

*"He who runs from God in the morning
will scarcely find Him the rest of the day."*

John Bunyan

Chapter Nine

It's Okay to Pray for Yourself

It's two months after my diagnosis. Both surgeries are behind me, and one chemo treatment is complete when my Uncle Ralph, who is 80 years old, sends me a message from his deathbed. He's been admitted to the hospital with breathing problems and within a week, to everyone's disbelief, he's gone. My parents visited him in the hospital several days before he died. With an oxygen mask on his face and unable to talk, he somehow communicated to my parents to provide him a pen and paper. On that piece of paper he wrote a message for them to deliver to me. In a very shaky cursive writing he wrote, "Tell Carol it is okay to pray for herself."

My parents deliver his note to me when I attend his memorial service. I unfold the piece of paper as I stand by myself in the church's sanctuary, amazed that one of his last earthly activities was to think about me. As I look down at his shaky handwriting, I wonder—have I been doing that? Have I allowed myself to pray for myself?

I fold the note into the palm of my hand throughout his memorial service, symbolically holding him close to me. I let his message work its way into my soul. Pray for myself? What does one do when one is praying for oneself? Isn't that like my plea-praying? Or is it something more profound?

To answer my question, I revisit my soul-searching. When I began this journey, I knew I needed something more—not just from God, but *with* God. I start looking for times where I can attempt quiet contemplation. I look for opportunities to sit outside, to observe God's world and the fact that I'm a part of that world, and instead of plea-praying to God, I start asking Him to join me. I find that when I truly quiet my mind and truly allow God's presence to appear, I can hear Him saying, "You are whole and complete, as I made you." Or, "Have faith that I am here with you." Most of the time, however, I simply feel His presence, because I allow Him to emerge.

I begin to realize that God exists within our spirit; His primary residence is inside the soul. My soul, your soul. He holds me up and fills me from within. It's up to me to take the time to place myself in a prayer state that invites His presence into my life. In my busy world of responsibilities of a job, wife, mother, friend and church member, I was missing out on this balance of spirit. I was missing out on quality time with God. My dear uncle's instructions, to pray for myself, to allow for that, is moving me toward a richer relationship with my Maker, the God Almighty, and my salvation.

 Revelations 3:20
Here I am! I stand at the door and knock. If any of you hears my voice and opens the door, I will come in and eat with you, and you with me.

"There's one thing about baldness, it's neat."

Don Herold

Chapter Ten

She's Bald

I'm attending a lunch presentation by the author of, *I Don't Know How She Does It*—testimony to how this busy, successful career woman, who is also a wife and mother, somehow manages to get everything done. She loses my attention when she divulges she has a nanny. I sit there politely looking her way as a few strands of my hair fall into my lap and wonder what her life would have been like if she'd not had that nanny and had been given the added responsibility of battling cancer. Selfish thoughts, I know, but damn it, my hair is falling out!

Now it's two days later and I'm heading to work, still with most of my tresses, but definitely some "thinning" upstairs. I know I'm precariously close to the end. Dr. Frenette had said two weeks, and it's been exactly two weeks since my first chemo treatment.

At my office I say hello and interact with several of the guys around the coffeepot, then proceed to my office to work on some projects needing my attention. A few hours later, as I often do out of habit, I reach up with my right hand and beginning at my lower neck just behind my ear, move my fingers up and through my hair. Except this time, when I pull my fingers back, I come away with a big glob of it. I stare at the glob for several seconds before reaching over and shaking it off my hand and into the wastebasket.

I repeat this "shedding process" numerous times throughout the remainder of the day, running my fingers up and through my scalp, and then dumping the remains into the trash basket. I wonder now and again about the poor person who empties our trashcans at night and what they will think about the long-haired, furry animal that obviously got loose in the office today.

I'm deep into this hair caress process, when Randy, a coworker I'd interacted with earlier in the morning, stops by and stands in my opened office doorway to talk about a project I'm working on. As he looks at me sitting at my desk about four feet away from him, he pauses in mid-sentence, gives me a curious look, and asks, "Did you get a haircut?"

"Nope." I then reach my fingers into my hair and give him a demonstration. His eyes go wide with shock, and he exits my doorway almost immediately, surely uncertain as to what to make of what he's just witnessed. I manage to laugh at his reaction, but mostly at the situation. It's absurd.

And, it's time. I have my hairstylist, Effie's, personal cell phone number, and permission to call her when I need it. We schedule an 8:00 p.m. appointment at her boutique. Tom and Lindsay go with me. How it happens that there's blessedly no one else at Effie's usually busy boutique, I cannot tell you, but there, under Effie's careful guidance, Lindsay takes the sheers and shaves my head. She's obviously enjoying herself immensely and watching her prevents me from going into the downward emotional spin that beckons.

The wig has been purchased already, so I place it on my head, and Effie fine-tunes it by trimming with her shears to shape it to my now bald head. Look at me! I have a new hairstyle! Two new hairstyles, if you count being bald. When we leave Effie and are getting into the car, Lindsay proclaims, "That was fun! When can I shave your head again, Mommy?" Leave it to a child to find the fun in cancer.

After we return home, I keep the wig on, trying to get used to the feel of it as we finish checking homework, watching TV, and closing out our day. Other than Lindsay and Tom providing occasional compliments on my new "do" our lives appear normal. But as I remove the wig for the evening, and place it on the Styrofoam stand on my dresser, I look at it and wonder how I've managed to get through this day.

The bald woman looking back at me in the mirror looks like a cancer patient. As long as I had hair, I could appear normal. Bald, I look like cancer. I want the normal me back. I'm tired, I'm scared, and I'm growing increasingly anxious with the whole situation.

What is happening to my physical body seems out of my control but to try to fight with animosity is futile. I resolve to acknowledge and allow this process to be what it is:

Difficult.

 1 Peter 5:7
Turn all your worries over to him. He cares about you.

You Will Need
Carol Fore Injaychock

A garden, able to grow
beneath gray skies.

It must be able to absorb the gloom of the rational emotions
Which are just as bleak as the irrational emotions.

The garden will need good dirt,
fertilized with love from friends
and strangers alike
who will turn the soil
keeping it nourished
with just enough nutrients.

The flowers will struggle through the chemo,
lose their petals,
yet still remain a flower.

A white wood picket fence surrounds the garden
With its gate, which doesn't creak.
Well, most of the time it doesn't creak.
The gate will allow loved ones, doctors and nurses, x-ray
technicians,
and an array of oncologists to enter.
They will treat the garden
Aiding and encouraging the floral buds to burst into full
bloom.

You will need a patio beside the garden
with a comfortable chair.
One where you can sit and rest to nurture the flowers
when they all emerge from the dark soil and bloom again.

You will open the white picket gate
and invite all your loved ones to enter
for a celebration.

They and you will rest on the patio
observing the garden that flourishes
beneath the sunshine that has been absent for too long.

"We are each of us angels with only one wing and we can only fly by embracing each other."

Luciano de Crescenzo

Chapter Eleven

Angels Among Us

A not so funny thing about these huge life battles: the little life battles don't stop while you take on the huge ones. There are still children to get ready for school, homework to help with, jobs to go to, marriages to work on, bills to pay. Life doesn't stop just so you can funnel all your strength into the huge thing. I'm learning that sometimes we need to allow others—those angels here on earth—to help us rescue ourselves.

Meg is one such angel and a counselor with the Blumenthal Cancer Center here in Charlotte. It seems to me that Meg's mission in life is to help as many cancer patients as she can. I met her briefly at the "Look Good, Feel Better" seminar I'd attended before I started chemo, and even then Meg knew better than I did that I would need ample ammunition for my emotional self as well. She reached out and nudged me toward what I didn't realize, on a conscious level, could help me.

With her soothing voice, she affirms that cancer is indeed a difficult journey and sometimes people need a place to talk about what's going on in their heads in a way that makes them feel like they're truly being heard. A place where thoughts and fears can be expressed and understood by others on the same journey. As I'm driving to a sales appointment, I talk to her on my cell phone and she invites me to the support group she facilitates.

My "normal self" immediately responds with, "I really don't want to be in a sad place where we talk about death and dying and cry a lot." Yet as soon as these words are out of my mouth, I have my "ah ha" moment. There it is again—the part of me that doesn't want to deal with death; doesn't want to think about dying. That little voice inside of me begins to scream, "Listen normal self! Things aren't normal anymore and you will need to do some abnormal stuff!" So I tell Meg, "I'll think about it. When do you meet?"

"Tuesdays at 6:30 p.m. in the Cancer Center's conference room," she says, adding, "and I hope to see you there."

At 6:30 p.m. on the Tuesday that follows the Thursday my hair disappears, I wear a soft black and white scarf on my head with a nice black hat to coordinate, and walk into a room full of strangers.

This first time in, I'm alone, by myself; no buddy to gain courage from. But I can do this, I think. I can be an extrovert. I have walked into social settings alone on more than one occasion. I learned a long time ago, if I wait until I have a buddy to do things with, it might take a while to find someone else who wants or needs to do the things I want or need to do. So here I am, and while it's certainly daunting to open that door to a group of strangers, it already feels like the best thing I've done in a long time.

Standing in the center of the small room is Meg and she's surrounded by several survivors of various cancers: non-Hodgkin lymphoma, lung, breast, ovarian, pancreas, and rectal. I already sense a common denominator amongst all of us; a shared desire to weather this journey with as much grace and courage as we can and to quiet the emotional head monsters that try to unsettle our spirits.

We sit in a circle; bookshelves on one side and a small sofa and multiple chairs lining the walls of the room. I learn that the size of the group can vary depending on how people are feeling. Or, unfortunately, on whether they're alive or not. One man travels to the group by city bus transportation since he can't drive due to side effects of his treatments. Some have to have friends or family bring them. Most of us drove ourselves, it seems. Meg decides to address the "elephant in the room," by saying, "The reality is, some sitting here right now will lose the war against this disease." As she says this, I anxiously look around at some who are nodding their heads with misty tears in their eyes, for they already know those who've lost the battle. I am, however, shocked at this proclamation. Thoughts in my head are screaming, "No! I can't handle the grief of getting to know people who will die! Wait, what if it's me?" There it is again—that initial belief that bad things happen to other people and then the realization that they can also happen to me.

Now Meg is asking us a "centering question" to "ground us in our thoughts," she explains.

"Tell me what you know for sure."

Silence.

Then, "What about this past week or day, brought enlightenment to you?"

One by one, each of us is to answer a question from the heart. Have you ever been in a circle of people where you were able to be real and honest about your life, knowing you would not be judged critically for your contribution? Where you could unfold your closely held linen napkin of beliefs, fears, and joys, laying it open for the observers to view the wrinkles that haven't quite pressed out as well as you would have liked?

It's a powerful, strengthening reservoir of companionship. Nowhere else in my life have I ever been with a more real group of people than those who were facing their own mortality. This group is a haven.

Thankfully, my support doesn't stop there.

It's October and I have two chemo rounds behind me. Chemo-induced menopause is setting in the day I arrive at our sales office and my emotions and raging hormones are erupting. I am decidedly out of synch so I sequester myself in my office just as I begin to lose control. Try as I may, I can't seem to reel things in; no matter my prayers, holding the bridge of my nose tightly, or taking deep breaths. Nothing is working. My coworker and friend, Wayne, stops in to say hello, and finds me just standing there, staring at the wall. He takes one look at my face and asks, "What's wrong?" I fall apart; big tears rolling down my face. I can't speak. I just stand there looking at him in desperation. I'm sure he thinks it's the cancer, and it is, but it would be just as accurate to say that I was losing it because of my screwed up hormones.

Wayne walks over and hugs me. Then, being a good friend, and a man unsure of how to deal with my emotional abyss, he leaves to retrieve reinforcements. And not just coworker reinforcements, but coworkers who can double as prayer warriors. In walks Wayne, Vern and Skip; men I've known for several years. Whatever they've been working on in their offices has been set aside without hesitation, for in what seems like less than two minutes since Wayne has left my office, they are all three standing beside me asking what they can do.

I know each of these men go to church and are Christians, but never would I have thought that what happens next is possible. One reaches for another's hand and mine, pulling us all together to form a circle. Skip, then Vern, then Wayne—each prays a prayer that lifts me up to the higher power we call God. I'm not sure what lifts me more, the fact they did this for me, or the effect the prayer has on me, which is a strong sensation that God's presence is in our sales office today.

Did a miracle happen and I'm put back together again and able to work? No. This Humpty Dumpty is still broken. I'm emotionally spent, but the cavalry has come in to try and save me and I relish that.

They all hug me after the prayers, and Vern, who is my boss, looks at me with concerned eyes and says, "Do what you need to do, Carol." I need to go home. Prayers aside, everyone will be better off for it.

Back at home on that pretty October, North Carolina day, with the sky crystal blue, the leaves all but fallen away, and the birds singing just to me, I begin closing the open windows of my house. Since we live on over an acre of land, our neighbors are not right next door to our house; however, the houses are within earshot of a good loud boisterous cry, and I was about to have a colossal one. I shut the windows as quickly as I can, bury my face into a sofa pillow in our living room, and begin not to weep, but to sob. The emotions start at the tip of my toes and emerge out through my entire body. I cry my darkened soul out. Everything within me physically shakes, and everything that is emotional, pours out. This is no sissy, let-some-steam-off cry. No siree, this is a much-needed, long-overdue, cleansing bawl.

My support group angels and now my coworkers have encircled me with love, giving me permission to be human with my anxiety; they have provided me with more gifts than I could have thought imaginable through their prayers and endearing concern. With their earthly presence, they help to remind me that I am not alone. God is indeed present and cry out to God I do. As the floodgates of my despair subside, I feel a much-needed peace and thankfulness for all the human angels in my life.

 Philippians 2:4
None of you should look out just for your own good. You should also look out for the good of others.

". . . but mostly, given another shot at life,
I would seize every minute . . .
look at it and really see it . . . and never give it back."

Erma Bombeck

Chapter Twelve

Chemo Update

E-mail to about 35 friends that I keep updated regularly—

Chemo Update
Sent: Friday, December 12th
Dear Friends,
Here's my chemo check-in update. I am doing okay. But, frankly this all SUCKS. That is about the only phrase I have to sum this up. If it weren't for all the friends that have sent cards, gifts, or have come to visit with and without food, it would have been very easy to go into a dark hole and give up. The chemo cure is truly a horrible way to have to go. I know you think I WILL get better, and I believe I will too. So that gives everyone a comfort zone, including me. But, the truth is, the shadow of the possibility of my dying is still a remote possibility and one that a cancer patient has to live with every day.

I am meeting people now, that I will end up going to their funerals no matter how hard the world and myself pray. What I pray for is for all of us to have the strength to endure, whatever the outcome is. I do believe I will get to see my daughter grow up, but I don't have 100% certainty with that belief. (None of us with or without cancer are guaranteed tomorrow). I believe that when I am through this phase of this journey, I will be a better person. When I ask people how they are, it won't be a passing social question. You become in tune to life and the pleasures of life that were just minor components of your day; now little things become a focal point. I watched a blue butterfly land on an orange flower in my backyard (before the frost hit) and savored that moment like never before in my past. I have more patience for obstacles in life. In the past, when I've run late for a meeting, or in getting Lindsay to school, I used to get totally frustrated. Guess what the worst case scenarios is? I'll be a little late. No one will die from it. So I don't fret so much.

The other night a man sang for my cancer support group. It was a Christmas song I had never heard before. When he was done I had tears in my eyes. I'm not sure why, other than the appreciation for this human being caring enough to come with his friend who is in remission; caring enough to sing a beautiful song about baby Jesus. I had a keen appreciation for his talent and for his being there. I hope I don't lose this new found sensitivity.

This latest chemo, yesterday, so far is proving to be less aggressive. I'm actually not nauseous at all. I'm a bit tired. The bone and body ache they say comes with this drug hasn't hit, and I'm hoping the Advil will ward that off. My blood count could drop again, but we are holding off on that expensive booster shot for now. The good news is, if I continue to feel no worse than this, I will probably move up the chemo schedule to every two weeks instead of three weeks. Next treatment is December 31st. Happy New Year! I told Tom I needed to let the folks know that work there in "The Drip Lounge" that they need to put a kaleidoscope ball in there that day so we can all party to the "drips." The not so good news is, what I thought was going to be radiation one time a week for six weeks, was a misunderstanding on my part. It's 30 treatments, five days a week for six weeks. GEEZ-LOUISE!!!!!! I started to throw something at Dr. Frenette when he told me that (I was laughing hysterically while I was attempting to throw, so he took it in good jest).

I am going to go to partial workdays starting next week. Actually, it will probably take me to Wednesday to get to that schedule, as I have work appointments Monday and Tuesday. I need to put me first and get home and do some walking to build myself up physically, as I really do get tired during the course of the days from the cumulative total effect of the chemo.

I appreciate everyone's support through all of this. I will never, ever be able to convey my depths of gratitude for all that you have meant to me through your e-mails, cards, gifts, telephone calls, and visits. It has truly been my lifeline. A letter was read in my support group last week that was written some 13 years ago by a cancer patient. A component of it was this, "You ask me what you can do for me. Keep reminding me of what I have to live for through your friendship and love." You have done that in so many ways.

When you pray, pray for a cure. If you knew that a daughter, wife, or mother would have to go through this, you would give ANYTHING for them not to have to endure this. This breast cancer is the #1 killer of women behind heart disease. And remember, you are not genetically safe. This is not in my direct line of family. 95% of cases are first time generations. Eat healthy, be leery of the medications you women take (my theory is the estrogen from birth control pills as estrogen feeds cancer and I was on them for 20 years) and exercise. Okay, I'll get off my soap box now. Thanks for allowing me to vent.

I hope the holidays are great for you and the new year is a HEALTHY year for us all.

Blessings to you this holiday season,
Carol I.

My friend Gretchen's response:

> Carol,
>
> Our philosophies are so tied into our experiences. I expect you will continue to have a keener appreciation for all the beauty around us and will remain focused on what is really important. I was just thinking the other day about how so many people don't look at the sky-don't wonder about the clouds--don't enjoy the sunrises and sunsets--don't look up as the geese fly over. These are some of the things that give our lives meaning...in my humble opinion!
>
> You continue to take care of you. You are sooooo right that none of us can be sure of seeing another sunset or sunrise, but facing the reality of an early death is too real. The rest of us can think about living for today but we can fool ourselves into believing that if we screw up today, we can fix it tomorrow. The real truth is we can only live in this very minute. And this very minute, I'm thinking of you and sending you my love and hope. It is good that you've given yourself the gift of your friends.
>
> Love to you,
> Gretchen

 Isaiah 42:16

So I will lead them along paths that they had not known before. I will guide them on roads they are not familiar with. I will turn the darkness into light as they travel. I will make the rough places smooth. Those are the things I will do. I will not desert my people.

"Adversity introduces a man to himself."

Unknown

Chapter Thirteen

Boomerangs

It's not until my third chemo treatment that the darkness of fear finds her. Usually I come home from treatments and function; it may be a slow mode function, but I generally do fine around Lindsay and Tom. But today I feel drained and without any energy, so I go straight to my bedroom to lay down on my bed. Lindsay comes into my bedroom and stands by my bedside. I look at her with concern. She lays her head on my chest, throws her arms around my neck, and soon I can feel the tears streaming down her cheek.

"Are you going to get better, Mommy?"

There's something about your heart getting caught in your throat that makes it hard to breathe. My spirit aches all the more knowing she is feeling sad for me.

"I believe I will, Lindsay," I say. "It's just that these treatments I'm taking are making my body tired." I hold her hand and try to return the conversation to the normalcy of her life, asking questions and talking about her school day. She stays with me for a while, not quite ready to release her grip on me.

My parents, for their part, are doing the best they can to place their fears and me in God's hands. That turning it over hasn't stopped their worry. They are mere mortals after all, but they are doing the best they know how to do.

I do my best to be in the Adult-Child mode, where I act more like an independent adult versus the dependent child I want to be. I mess up at least once. There's a spot on a thigh bone and I have to go to yet another doctor, a specialist, not just any average doctor, to have it checked. This has me worried to maximum worry-levels. I come home from my initial specialist's visit with copies of my X-rays. The spot is blaring at me and the specialist can't say whether it is or isn't cancer. "We'll have to watch it for the next several weeks and see if it grows." I have just arrived home and am looking at my X-rays, when my dad calls.

"How are you doing, sweetheart?"

"I'm not sure how I am." A child is not supposed to lie to their parent, are they? "I've got a spot on my thigh bone and it could be the cancer has already spread there. The doctor doesn't know for sure."

As soon as that confession blurts out of my mouth, I realize how bad I have just slipped up.

My dad asks several questions to clarify where it is, how big it is, and what do they think it might be. I give him as much consolation as I can to remedy my confession.

"Dad, I have no pain, I can walk on my leg, there's been no difference in the questionable leg versus my other one. I'm sure this is all going to be fine."

My rationalizations, optimistic as I'm trying to be, don't give him much, if any, peace of mind. We end our conversation with my promise to keep them posted. After we hang up, I hold the phone in my hand contemplating what's just happened. I'm not certain whether I feel worse about the spot on my bone or having told my parents more than they might be able to handle. I gave my dad way more information than I should have before I knew for sure what we were dealing with. I knew he'd now worry enough for both of us.

I go to follow-up visit number one with the specialist. No change. I make an immediate telephone call to my parents.

"All is looking well. No change in the spot. It will be fine, I'm sure."

There are several more weekly follow-up visits, followed by more phone calls with the "no change" status report. Finally, after numerous weeks of this, the doctor specialist resolves that the spot is just a spot, nothing more.

It's a difficult balance beam to walk; this protecting our loved ones; wanting not to be a burden, yet still having needs. Like dodging boomerangs, all day long.

And the thing about boomerangs—they keep coming. Seemingly out of nowhere, wham, something else hits.

Boomerang #1: When the doctors feared my cancer had already spread, but couldn't decide if the place toward the back of my armpit, right at my lymph nodes, was where it had spread to, or was starting from. If it had spread already, I was in for a dire prognosis.

Boomerang #2: That spot on my thighbone. "Possible cancer," they'd said. The look of fear in the X-ray technician's eyes as she looked from the scans to me said it all. I was done for. Turns out, after several months of "watching" that spot through on-going X-rays, it was decided it was what it was, a spot on my bone. Modern technology is teaching us new things about our bodies. One of which is, our bones often have markings, sort of like birthmarks.

Boomerang #3: A bleeding rectum. Again, they fear it might be colon cancer. A colonoscopy is added to my regime, just what I need to add to the "fun" I'm already having. What a relief when they discover it's only hemorrhoids.

Boomerang #4: Cysts on my liver. The various scans keep turning up things on my body. There are spots on my liver that have to be checked out, and with more scans and X-rays they finally determine they're nothing to be worried about, just "simple" cysts. Simple, maybe, but they've caused another round of distress through the journey.

Boomerang #5: A mammogram is done to establish a new baseline to which all future mammograms will be compared. It's not supposed to be a big deal. Go in, have the mammogram. The new photos will then be on file for all other mammograms to be compared to. Wait. What? A spot on my other breast? That boomerang hits me upside the head, makes a U-turn, then hits me again. This may be the most difficult hurdle thus far ...

I'm well into my treatments now; just a couple of weeks prior to Christmas when I get that news. It's not a good thing when you're currently in chemo treatments and more cancer is discovered. Not good. Not good at all. It's the holidays, for goodness sake! This is supposed to be a happy time and I. Am. Not. Happy.

I reach out to my friend, Melissa. She's a minister and works as a hospital chaplain with cancer patients. I tell her about the latest development.

"How do I go on?" I ask. To be honest, I don't think I really expect her to know, I just need to talk to a friend, and someone I view as having a better connection with God then myself. Melissa comforts me with friendship words, tells me she will pray for me, and she gives me a thin book to read. It's a book that a minister wrote about losing his young child to cancer, she explains. The reality is, the child will die. Now I know what you're probably thinking—that's not much comfort, and you'd be right, but not completely right. Getting to acceptance of life's darkness and the reality of dying is sometimes where we must be to truly live.

The book gives me a gift of scripture from Isaiah 40. This scripture has two subtitles. The first is, "Comfort through trust in the Lord." Isaiah 40:29 "He giveth power to the faint; and to them that have no might he increaseth strength."

The second is, "The majesty of the Lord." vs 31 "But they that wait upon the Lord shall renew their strength; they shall mount up with wings as eagles; they shall run, and not be weary; and they shall walk, and not faint."

Strength enough to walk without fainting—strength to get up if I do. That becomes my creed. I just want strength—enough.

Waiting on the biopsy result is grueling. The results take four days and over a week since the doctor has said, "With your history, we just can't be sure of what it is." Yet three days before Christmas, I receive the best gift I ever remember receiving; a phone call with a happy lady on the other end of the phone. She tells me, "The spot on the breast is nothing more than a small cyst; nothing at all to be alarmed about!" My knees buckle and I literally collapse to the floor from relief. I prayed for strength to get me through the grueling wait; NOW I am going to collapse at good news? We are strange species, we humans.

I celebrate Christmas in a special way this year. I celebrate being alive. I still have my eyelashes and eyebrows. I'm halfway through my chemo treatments. There's enough energy most days to be active and to conduct my normal routines. I'm filled with the joy and peace of the season, yet, had I been able to look farther down the road, I might have been full of dread.

 Psalm 30:10-12
Lord, hear me. Show me your favor. Lord, help me. You turned my loud crying into dancing. You removed my black clothes and dressed me with joy. So my heart will sing to you. I can't keep silent, Lord, my God, I will give thanks forever.

*"To liberate the human spirit
we must embrace heightened consciousness
and enhance the flow of positive energy.
We are beings of light and energy,
once we accept this truth
our soul can soar with the angels."*

Micheal Teal

Chapter Fourteen

Heavenly Angels

My experience has taught me that heavenly angels don't necessarily show up in our lives dressed in white with large wings hanging off of their backs. But that doesn't mean that they're not hovering nearby.

It's late January and the latest chemo drug, Taxol, is being dripped into my veins every three weeks. This one, which is supposed to be easier on me, hits me harder than a ton of bricks and leaves me listless and lethargic. I feel too awful to work or participate in anything. I stay in bed most days. To suggest I am melancholy would be putting it mildly. Not feeling well for multiple days on end is taking its toll, and I am depressed.

After about three weeks of this horrible time, there is a morning I manage to get out of bed and dress for the day in a sweatshirt, blue jeans, tennis shoes, and my favorite multicolored cotton bandanna covering my bald head. My daughter is at school and my husband at work, so I sit on the edge of my bed thinking I'm alone in the house. I'm just sitting there in an unintentional prayer position, holding my bowed head in my hands as I begin to cry. I have a broken spirit, I'm tired, and life feels bleak. I want to have my normal life back. I have another two months before the chemo will be finished, and radiation to begin thereafter. Large crocodile tears stream down my cheeks as I hold onto the end of my emotional rope. My broken spirit pleads and beseeches God for the strength to go on.

I sit on the edge of my bed for several minutes, in an emotional abyss of chemo-generated darkness. I'm not going anywhere, I'm not expecting any activity, other than the streaming tears to occur—least of all what happens next.

Suddenly I sense I'm not alone; she's there beside me, just to my left. I can't see her with my eyes, but I "see her" with my spirit. I lean over and as she puts her arm around me, I fold into her. She holds me up and caresses my spirit with her love. I am weak physically, but somehow this moment brings strength to my weary soul.

Virginia Radford is here and she's saying, "You can do this, Carol. It won't be easy, but you can do this."

Her visit doesn't last long; a moment, really. I question if it happened at all. Yet, had she not been there, when I folded into her, I would have surely fallen over onto the bed. Had she not been there, my spirit would not have found the nourishment that it needs this morning. It was too real to be imagined and I don't believe I have the capability for that kind of vivid imagining.

Virginia was an inspiration to me during my youth, just by the way she lived her life. She could have easily chosen to function with a poor, pitiful me attitude through her earthly battle with cancer. I'm thankful she chose to have a positive outlook on life. She battled the battle many years but lost the war much sooner than her husband and her young daughters would want. While she was with us, she lived her life for others to witness. She didn't close me out because I was a young girl that wouldn't understand. Her life, filled with cancer for years, not months, was a positive testimony. Learn from it I did. When it was time to invoke the lessons she had instilled in me, she found a way to remind me of her wisdom. She was an angel of love while she was on this earth, and now an angel of love and rejuvenation for me during my own cancer journey.

"Thank you, Virginia," I say aloud. "I am indebted to you this morning and I won't let you down."

Exodus 23:20-21

I am sending an angel ahead of you. He will guard you along the way. He will bring you to the place I have prepared. Pay attention to him. Listen to what he says. Do not refuse to obey him. He will not forgive you if you turn against him. My very Name is in him.

*"When you get into a tight place
and everything goes against you
until it seems that you cannot
hang on for a minute longer,
never give up then,
for that is just the place and time
when the tide will turn."*

Harriet Beecher Stowe

Chapter Fifteen

Snow Storms

I've had the date circled and highlighted on my calendar for weeks now—February 26th. Written in bold ink are the words, LAST CHEMO TREATMENT! This is to be my first-day-of-the-rest-of-my-life date. It's the date I've anticipated and yearned for; to finally get the last treatment finished and over with. I have visualized leaving the medical office building where my infusions happen, and see myself with my mind's eye physically pushing the glass swinging doors open, feeling the excitement as I depart from The Drip Lounge for the last time. Done - Done - Done will be the dance I will dance.

Tom is my official chauffeur and chemo lounge escort for the day. He wants to be with me for this last treatment. He has to return home from his work, which is a 45-minute normal drive time, to retrieve me from our house to take me to my 1:00 p.m. appointment.

The snowstorm, the one that will leave about six inches in our area and other parts of the southeast, hits about the same time Tom leaves his office. An hour later, he's still trying to make it to me. I call the oncologist's office to make sure they are still operating and that I can still come even though it's looking like I'll be a little late. I'm told to come on; that they're staying open. Tom's 45-minute drive has turned into an almost two-hour one and when I see his vehicle pull into our driveway, I hang my head, admitting defeat. The roads are just too treacherous. I am battling cancer; I don't want to die in a traffic accident.

I stand at my living room window looking out on the beautiful, hideous snowfall. The crocodile tears escape down my cheek as my nine-year-old daughter, who is witnessing my anguish, wraps her arms around my waist and tries to offer me some comfort. I love her for that, but still feel horrible. It's not supposed to happen this way! This was supposed to be my victory dance day, of Done - Done- Done; instead it's a defeated dance of - Why? Why? Why? Today of all days. This day, the one I have proclaimed and circled on my calendar as my day. Instead it belongs to the snow.

I call my oncologist's office to reschedule. They give me a new date, a week away. I write the new date on my calendar, but not written as bold as the original date has been. I have been knocked down once and don't trust that I won't be knocked down again.

It's a heartache of all heartaches to be so close to the finish line and you just can't cross.

The snow has won today's battle, but I am determined to win the war.

Now, one week later, and with the snow melted and my world looking like a beautiful sunshine-filled day, I walk out of The Drip Lounge for the last time. I give the physical push of those glass doors and feel an unexpected mix of emotions. Relief is there, but suddenly, there are other confusing emotions as well. Like fear and insecurity. The chemo treatments were evidence I was physically in the fight. As long as the treatments occurred, I was participating in something to kill this disease. I saw my oncologist on a regular basis and he gave me regular reports. Now, the activity and regular visits with the oncologist would not be as frequent.

Had the chemo done its job?

How would I know?

Only time will tell.

 Psalm 46:1

God is our place of safety. He gives us strength. He is always there in times of trouble.

A Perfect Day
Carol Fore Injaychock

Waking Up.

Nothing Hurts.

Taste buds work.

Energy enough.

No treatments scheduled.

Arrival of a card in the mailbox.

Shining Sun.

Singing birds.

Tail wagging dog.

Lunch with a friend.

Feeling of Inner Peace.

*"Since you get more joy out of giving joy to others,
you should put a good deal of thought
into the happiness that you are able to give."*

Eleanor Roosevelt

Chapter Sixteen

Life is a Two-Way Street

Surgery. Check.

Chemo. Check.

All that's left now is radiation.

To prepare, I have to make a visit to the "tattoo parlor" at the radiology medical office. There they mark the alignment places with small tattoo spots; souvenirs for life.

They mark me up with felt tip markers, putting "x's" on numerous spots across my chest. I look like a tic-tac-toe board when they finish and I'm instructed to avoid allowing them to wash off when I shower. It takes three trips for them to have the markings and my alignment template complete. The daily routine of radiation begins in late March, and lasts a very long six weeks.

The calls, cards, letters, and e-mails, slow to a trickle. To the outside world, I'm done with the worst part of the war, yet my reality is, while I'm close to signing my name on the end of the treaty, I haven't sat down to the final negotiations yet.

Every single day, except for Saturday and Sunday, I put my weary body into my car and drive myself to the hospital. The radiation takes less than 30 minutes from the time I park, make my way into the hospital, undress, get zapped, dress again, visit with the friendly nurses, and return to the parking lot. After I get home my best friend is fast becoming my sofa. It hugs me close. My aunt's homemade quilt, the one I've had for years, exerts all the love it can muster from its worn threads to comfort me as I fold it up and over my tired, aching body.

Mid-way through treatments, I receive an invitation to go to the beach for a long weekend with women from my Sunday school class. The timing is perfect. My doctor is okay with me missing one day; I can make it up on the end of the process. He tells me to go, with his blessing.

There are about 15 of us together for the weekend at a beach house. I relish being with all these ladies I've known for several years; those who have helped me through the cancer journey with their gifts of friendship and food deliveries. And thankfully, cancer is not a dominant component of the conversation. I'm here to relax and enjoy their friendships and not put a dark cloud over the weekend.

In truth, I have made myself go on this weekend trip. It was organized by someone else, with invitations extended to the entire class. I was responsible for making myself available and taking advantage of the invitation. I could have easily said, "Woe is me. Nobody cares," and stayed with my sofa and quilt for comfort. It's a two-way street from my perspective. I had an invitation. I needed to choose whether I would wait for someone to call and say, "Oh, I do hope you can come!" Or, without any prodding, I could say, "Thanks for the invite, I plan to be there! Wig, short hair, fatigue and all!"

Don't go away, I want to say—those of you on the friendship side of this cancer equation. Stay engaged in the process as best you can. It's not over until it's completely over and even then, it's still not done.

Don't go away, cancer patient. Don't go away from life. Don't stop embracing it. Keep moving forward. Accept invitations. Make telephone calls or e-mails when those don't come to you. It is a two-way street. All of life is. Travel your side of the road towards caring relationships.

You will bless them.

They will bless you.

Matthew 7:12

In everything, do to others what you would want them to do to you.
This is what is written in the Law and in the Prophets.

Life's unfairness is not irrevocable;
we can help balance the scales for others,
if not always for ourselves."

Hubert Humphrey

Chapter Seventeen

Disability

Statistics tell us that one out of three people will develop cancer in their lifetime; one out of eight women will have breast cancer. Then there are other things–heart attacks, other diseases. Are you like me and believe that "it's not in my family," and put off scheduling the needed doctor appointment? Are you young, so you believe if it does happens, it's still a long, long way off?

When cancer happened in my life, I already had some financial planning in place: a will, life insurance policy, a personal disability policy, and one through my employer. Having these benefits in place brought me some comfort and I was grateful for being prepared.

Just after New Year's I had decided to go on full disability, and stopped work completely. The treatments had taken their toll and I wasn't able to continue. Based on my tenure, there was full pay for a few weeks, but that payout diminished when I reached the point where Long Term Disability group insurance started, which is 60% of my salary. The insurance company is the dictating entity of what is paid out, based on its agreement with my employer. While they love to fly blimps over major sports event, I discovered they were not very pleased with having to serve my income needs. What they are interested in, is my returning to work as soon as their schedule dictates.

My primary oncologist has documented in my medical notes that my return to work should be delayed until at least mid-August. My new doctor, however, the one administering my radiation treatments, writes my situation up in my medical file as doing "okay" and connects my fatigue to lack of sleep due to hot flashes. The insurance company's guidelines mandate that "four weeks after treatments, the patient should return to work." That means that they want me to be back at work in late June. That's less than a month away and my body is absolutely not close to being ready for that schedule.

I had sent in the required standard forms to the insurance company to initiate my long-term disability. Yet, after leaving several voicemail messages in their company mailbox, I still haven't received a response.

With determination to speak to someone "live," I navigate through their convoluted voicemail prompts until I finally get a real person on the line. I explain to the customer representative, who serves the mighty blimp marketing machine, that I need to confirm receipt of my forms and the continuation of my disability income benefits.

"Your medical documentation by your latest doctor indicates you are fine," she says, in a condescending tone. Then she proceeds to read to me the doctor's notes indicating my noted fatigue associated with hot flashes.

I rub my bandanna-covered head, look in the mirror of my den I am sitting in, and see my weak eyes staring back at me, wondering why the doctor hadn't seen my weakness and known I wasn't just suffering from hot flashes?

"You have no serious symptoms based on your last medical record report. Therefore, your benefits will stop at week four since your last treatment."

She, this voice on the other end of the phone and her blimpy company, doesn't give a damn. Her voice feels cruel.

"Is there anything else?" she asks.

With angry, frustrated tears in my eyes, I respond with a very flippant response.

"I hope you are never on this end of the phone struggling and needing insurance and get what you are giving me." I slam down the phone. She doesn't hear the slam (I hope), but it feels good.

 Proverbs 31:8-9
Speak up for those who can't speak for themselves. Speak up for the rights of all those who are poor. Speak up and judge fairly. Speak up for the rights of those who are poor and needy.

*"Start by doing what's necessary;
then do what's possible;
and suddenly you are doing the impossible."*

St. Francis of Assisi

Chapter Eighteen

Completion of Treatments

From my journal:

5/17/04: Friday, 5/14 was my last radiation treatment. As I laid there on that radiation table the tears started to form. I hugged those two nurses when I was done and told them I hoped they would not be busy in the future. My meaning was not lost on them. My hope is that fewer people will have cancer, fewer needing treatment. When I got home, I sat on the edge of my bed and bawled. The tears are in my eyes as I write this. So much emotion that I'm not sure has any one identifying adjective. It's so much - the length of time, the marathon, the fears, the blessings, the friendships cultivated and lost, the new found strength, the weaknesses, the loss of the old me, the gain of the new me. It is so much good and so much awful. It's over in so many ways, but never truly ever completely over. I look to the future and am blurred by the vision. I can't see exactly where I'm going. Will the future be short or long? Will it have a job that fulfills me? Will I be different in attitude of life? I think I will be. I want to believe life will hold some positives for me, for my family. We deserve it. But, that doesn't mean it will happen. One foot in front of another. Make a plan, but don't plan on the plan. Be flexible. Enjoy the ride - even the hard times are times. Times to be relished as part of the journey, strengthening character, building us into who we are supposed to be. I don't believe God gives us these awful things that happen to us. He may very well know they're going to happen. But to believe He causes cancer in my life, or causes a child to be born deformed is not what I believe. I believe bad things happen to good people because of life.

I believe God takes those heartaches and problems and uses them to a better good. What we have to do is Let Go and Let God. That has been my mantra through all of this. I've done that at times, but not always. Being human, I've tried to deal with this in a stubborn, prideful, human way. God's strength is how I manage to smile. When I let go and let God, the peace is there. I want to form this plan, but I need to allow God to have the final say. I just hope I can hear Him speaking when it's the right time.

The next weeks are crucial—ob-gyn appointment, mammogram appointment, orthopedic appointment, and in early July I see my surgeon. Once I'm through all those, I'll breathe a sigh of relief. Then I'll be anxious for the next two years as recurrence is highest in those first two years. I hope I have the same outcome as my mentors Jan, Anne, and Holly; all are still cancer-free and smiling.

The journey has been tough. I didn't think I could do this, and I have. That makes me proud of myself. But I didn't do it without the support primarily of Tom. He has truly walked beside me through this. And the food, prayers, e-mails that have come from my church, St. John's, even those who were strangers have become strong supporters. It's time to gain back my strength, say a lot of "thank you's" and begin to pay it forward …

 Psalms 61:2

From a place far away I call out to you. I call out as my heart gets weaker. Lead me to the safety of a rock that is high above me.

*"To be what we are,
and to become what we are capable of becoming,
is the only end of life."*

Robert Louis Stevenson

Chapter Nineteen

Emerging

From the beginning I vowed to beat the breast cancer beast, and to honor that thought process, I created the proverbial carrot on the end of the stick—something to look forward to when the treatments were over. I needed a place that would feed my soul. I had visited that place when I was fourteen-years-old with my family—Yosemite National Park. Even though I was young when I had my original visit, I very much appreciated the beauty of that place. The enormous redwood trees and spectacular waterfalls exuded beauty everywhere and I think of that place as my version of the Garden of Eden.

One month after my treatments end in late June, with minimal hair growth covering my head, Tom, Lindsay, and I, fly to San Francisco, California. We rent a car to take us the rest of the distance to the park.

We drive into Yosemite on a sunshine, cloudless blue-sky day that has a hint of coolness. I need a lightweight jacket. Our welcoming committee consists of two coyotes trotting toward us side by side with their tongues hanging out, looking worn and tired. They look straight at me and seem to give a nod in my direction as though they acknowledge my arrival—me, another species, worn and tired. They are oblivious to the gawking tourists that maneuver around them in the many vehicles. Nor are they traumatized by the shrill of my daughter's excited voice screeching, "Look, Daddy!"

We walk the trails to view the falls: Bridal Veil, Venereal, and Yosemite. All beautiful, just as I remember. From the mountaintops, they shower the landscape. Their tumultuous roar, as they fall over their high cliffs, fills my being with their enormous strength. I allow them to wash my soul and spirit with their beauty.

In this area, the glaciers of the past have formed, developed, and penetrated. When the days of the ice age were over, the mountains of El Capitan and Half Dome rose from the basin like kings to stand over this majestic park. These mountain kings now tower over us with their smooth and molded beauty, glistening in the sun. The sun glows upon them, reflecting its rays upon their mammoth sides, warming them to the day. At sunset, Half Dome glistens with an amber glow under the sun's final rays of the day. The stars and moon then rise to take the sun's place as they reflect upon these kings.

Mirror Lake is the primary spot I want to visit before the end of our first day in the park. I remember how the mountain behind it glistened and reflected in the lake. We've seen much already the first part of our day but I need to get to this area before the sun begins its descent. I need to get to the lake. As we walk up the final pathway towards the water, Tom turns and says to me, "Slow down, we aren't in a hurry."

But, I am. Why? I'm not sure. I have been to this place in my dreams, many times. Maybe I feared I'd never make it back. I need to hurry before something sweeps me away before I can see it again. More than anything, I want to see my daughter in this place.

What is it about Mirror Lake? Is it how it reflects its surroundings that so intrigues me? The reflection of a 14-year-old girl who once was here?

We arrive at the lake's edge to see a shallow, small body of water nestled in a green meadow area. The water of the "lake" is only ankle deep, no more than that in depth, but still beautiful. We stand there for a long while. I sit with Tom on a large boulder, watching Lindsay laugh at herself as she walks in the "lake" with the appearance that she's walking on water. She is glowing.

I have arrived. We have arrived together. We have experienced much in this day of renewal. The waterfalls have fallen around me and have cleansed my spirit. The gleaming sun has warmed me. Tom and Lindsay, who have endured much with my struggle, are here with me enjoying the reflection of the beauty around us. We spend time reflecting on our lives and how precious life is. We have come full circle. The girl of fourteen, now 45, has seen much, and like El Capitan and Half Dome, I have been shaped and formed by the journey.

On Day Two of our trip, we travel to just beyond the valley floor of Yosemite, to Mariposa, an area where mammoth redwoods reside. When we make the turn into the park, there, filling up my entire peripheral vision, is nothing but the base of a tree, and that isn't the largest one. Here, too, I visited as a teenager. My older brother and younger sister and I held hands and chained ourselves together in front of the largest tree, appropriately named, "Grizzly." With arms extended as far apart as we could stretch, we held each other's hands, the three of us barely stretching our bodies across this tree's base. The trunks reach up and out toward the clear California sky.

Lindsay dubs them the "broccoli trees." Large, tall red stalks with toppings of green broccoli. I'm amazed at their grandeur. Like the majestic kings of El Capitan and Half Dome, they persevere. They endure.

Mother Nature has invoked much hardship here; hardship that has molded and changed the shape of the area. Here, God has been at work. Everything perfectly molded and formed according to God's plan and evolved from a wonderful majestic manifestation of His glory.

Harsh as it's been, this cancer journey has shaped me, too, and the remains of what transpired over time has left me with a new strength and resilience. I don't feel as strong as those kings and redwoods yet, but I do feel smoothed and caressed where I once was held hostage by fear. Like those stoic redwoods, rising and stretching as far up to the sky as possible, enduring, I'm spreading my roots deep down into the ground to find firm footing. I'm trusting that my God is shaping me for things unknown to me, but known, blessedly, to Him, and for now, that is enough.

 Colossians 1:11
We want you to be very strong, in keeping with his glorious power.
We want you to be patient. Never give up. Be joyful.

Time

Carol Fore Injaychock

Time – is there plenty? Ask someone diagnosed with cancer.

Time – The clock softly ticks off the seconds methodically in its
soothing tone.

The shower hums through the pipes of the house lingering
longer than mandated

The dog laps up his water with numerous leisurely slurps,
as if in no hurry to finish.

The coffee pot perks its soon to be savored coffee at
a soothing pace

The darkness of the morning eases away slowly, before
giving way to the light.

The school bus picks up its designated riders hurriedly at
the street

The office workers make their commute to be at the awaiting
desk at the appointed
Time.

Time – It's an all important thing that we wrap our days around.

Time – It is not tangible – or is it?

Time – We have it on our hands.

Time – It propels us towards goals.

Time – It reflects in the mirror, where once a younger appearance
stared back at us.

Time – It shocks us by the evolving toddler who suddenly is a
teenager.

Time – Is it friend or foe?

Time – Moves slow and quick, simultaneously.

Time – We feel it on a leisure spring warm afternoon as we savor
the sun on our face and we give thanks to it for the reprieves
it provides.

Time – Creates conflicts and stress as we rush to the appointed
meeting or deadline.

Time – We are amazed we can't find all that we need.

Time – It is a gift to us.

Time – It is precious.

Time – Is there plenty?
Ask a cancer survivor.

Reflections

*"Everything that happens to you
is your teacher.
The secret is to learn
to sit at the feet of your own life
and be taught by it."*

Polly B. Berends

Chapter Twenty

What I've Learned

Imperfect as it was, my life, just before my cancer diagnosis, looked like a "perfectly normal" life.

Sure, I worked a sales job in Charlotte, North Carolina that had "miserable" written at the top of the job description. While I loved the co-workers in my home office, the management team, out of Atlanta, had taken over a few months prior to my diagnosis, and believed in motivation by intimidation. It was standard operating procedure for the Atlanta-based Vice President to call my immediate boss, who worked at the Charlotte location with me, and begin the conversation by cussing. This environment was toxic to all of us on the Charlotte team. But it was a job, and despite it all, I was grateful to have it.

My marriage was struggling and my husband and I were in counseling to improve our relationship.

I was deep in the busyness of being a proud mother of an elementary school fourth grade daughter. There was a regular supply of school, church and basketball activities to keep up with and functions to attend on a regular basis.

While I had a religious and spiritual background, looking back, I didn't realize I was traveling the road of life without an efficient GPS or a good map to tell me which direction I needed to go; that I was actually lost in the turmoil and busyness of it all. I was bumping along the road with its numerous crevices and potholes when I fell into the crater of a cancer diagnosis.

The diagnosis felt unfair; it came along at a really lousy time.

Why is it another crisis will occur when one or more are already going on; is there a negative activity magnet in our lives? I didn't have time for any of it. Or did I?

It's been nine years since that day and much has changed.

***

I've been working on this book off and on for the past several years. The resistance to write about my journey was great. It was difficult to re-visit the experience; I wanted to leave the unpleasantness of the entire trip behind. Forget. Move on. Get back to "normal." Whatever normal is. It took effort to look back; to read over the details that were logged in the journal I kept during the treatments; the journal which sat dormant for so long on my bedside table. I resisted opening the slim blue and white volume, seemingly unable to allow myself to go down that memory lane. But something was calling me back.

One day I picked it up from my nightstand, and moved it to our coffee table in the living room. I treated it like a magazine I would lay aside to await my leisure reading. Over the course of the next several days, I continued to glance in its direction, but not open it up. It was like a long lost enemy that I needed to confront. Finally, one evening when my family was out and I was alone, I opened it and read it cover to cover. Hard. Difficult. Wrenching. There were many points during the reading that my chest heaved as I struggled to breathe. Especially challenging was reading about those gloomy January days; of being in bed and my body giving out on me.

Yet I was reminded of all those who loved me through those hard times. I was reminded of holding hands with my co-workers, Vern, Wayne, and Skip in my office as they circled around me and each prayed. It was an experience like none I've ever had before in a workplace or a church. As I poured over the memories, it was the people—my human angels—the ones who helped me through some of my darkest hours, who reappeared in my thoughts. Dread was replaced with gratitude, as I loved them from this new me, letting them into my psyche to again take a special place in my heart.

As I revisited that journal, and my journey, I realized that sometimes we need to remember, even if it is painful. Lessons, if we allow them, will continue to evolve. Insights appeared that I didn't see clearly when I first wrote them.

I have been changed by this experience. Today I am more proactive about keeping my life's valve open, as a serendipitous moment is always possible. I aspire to let life in, whether it be letting a song on the radio "speak" to me, or acknowledging that a simple smile from the man or woman riding the elevator with me is a blessing in my day. I still have a long way to go, but the gifts of introspection and gratitude are gifts gained by my cancer journey. Maybe, just maybe, without cancer I would have gotten to this stage of desire for a fuller life. I don't believe, however, it would ever have been as profound.

 1 Thessalonians 5:18
Give thanks no matter what happens. God wants you to thank him because you believe in Christ Jesus.

"The Past is strapped to our backs.
We do not have to see it, we can always feel it."

Mignon McLaughlin

Chapter Twenty-One

Acceptance

In the years since my diagnosis, I've counseled many friends who have been affected by cancer, either through their own diagnosis or because of someone they love. Not long ago, an elderly friend, diagnosed about a year prior, sat beside me in a quiet hallway of the church we both attend. Her hair was thinned by the chemo to a fuzzy covering; she had blisters in her mouth and pain in her bones. The doctors had recently told her, "There is nothing more we can do."

She looked at me and took a deep breath, surely to fight back the tears. As they escaped down her cheek, I wiped them gently away with as much tenderness in my touch as I could.

With a desperate plea in her voice, she asked, "When will I accept this?" She was 79 years old, had lived in Brussels, Belgium, New York City, and finally settled in Charlotte, North Carolina. Her life had been difficult after her husband abandoned her, but she'd raised her only child, a daughter, with the assistance of family members. I'm amazed that she was never bitter over what should have been. She was happy with her life. It had been filled with much: church leader, business woman, friend, and mother. Her personality and life exuded sweetness and goodness. She was a generous person, giving of herself and talents in our church and in the community. She had touched many lives, mine included. She wanted her life to continue. Of course she did.

I reached out to hold her hand, uncertain of the words, if there were any, that could help with the moment.

Sitting there next to her, grasping for the proper words to say, my thoughts reached back to my own journey towards acceptance of this cancer card that, in the game of life, is really nothing short of a Joker's Wild. During my treatments, there was a period when I began to believe that things weren't going to end well; when it seemed that creatures from Harry Potter's Hogwarts world, the dementors, had arrived to suck the life out of me. Days I was so weakened by the treatments that I couldn't get out of bed. My husband managed to get our daughter to school and kept our schedules normal. My "new normal" was aches from the treatments, blisters in my mouth, and being and feeling weak. Until I experienced it, I had never envisioned it would or could get as bad as it did. The weather and my mood were dreary. My normal optimistic self went into hiding. My daughter's pictures when she was about six weeks old and another from her kindergarten year stared back at me from the shelf just across from my bed. At the time of my darkest days, just after the new year, she was just nine years old and in the fourth grade. Let me live to see her through middle school, I pleaded to the bleakness. To be honest, I preferred seeing her through college, but I didn't want to risk being too greedy with my request.

In the latter part of that January, one of my best friends, Betsy, called to ask if she and her husband, Bobby, could bring by some food for us. This motivated me to get out of bed and dress in something extravagant; blue jeans and a sweatshirt were a major improvement from my pajamas. When they arrived, I begged them to stay and eat with us. Betsy had prepared a wonderful pasta dish. My blistered mouth enjoyed the soft coolness of the pasta. We conversed about general things, the dreary weather, Bobby's job search, and other normal life stuff. We were careful to stay away from negative cancer dialogue. Betsy had known me about the longest of any of my adult life friends. She sat across from me at our dinner table that night, with tears in the edges of her eyes. She was trying hard to be brave for me. I felt a stab of guilt for causing her heart and this evening to be sad for her.

Their visit lasted a little more than an hour. When they made preparations to leave, I walked them to the front door and hugged them tight, as though they were my lifeline and as I closed the door behind them, I held on to the brass doorknob and leaned my forehead into the wood of the door.

"God," I prayed, "I sure would like to have a happy dinner with my friend in the near future. Please let me get better." I knew my friends were on the other side of that door asking the night stars, "Is she going to die?" I looked like I was knocking on death's door; I felt like I was knocking on death's door. Strength enough to take a step without fainting was about all I had, not much more. It was the closest to death I would ever feel and come.

So, as I looked into my elderly friend eyes, and saw her facing her own mortality, I wondered if I had anything to offer. Anything to give. It's fact that we all are going to leave this human life behind sooner or later. Some of us will have long full lives; some of us long not-so-full lives; some of us short full lives; some of us short not-so-full lives. But I also knew that she wasn't ready to go yet; that she wasn't ready to leave her daughter even though her daughter was grown.

Holding my dear elderly friend's hand, I took in a deep breath and exhaled. Then I tried to share my thoughts on acceptance.

"When I looked at death closer than I wanted to," I started, "I didn't want to accept I would die, but what I managed to do, the best my human abilities allowed, was turn it over to God. I was feeling like there were two of me: my normal self, and my cancer self. I allowed those two selves to fold into each other and then let God embrace them both with His love and grace. In time I began to sense His presence and had the belief that He would provide the love and support my daughter and family and friends would need should I not survive." I paused and added, "Your daughter will be okay; you will be okay."

I realized, as I held my friend's hand, that through reflection, prayer, God's grace, and love from family and friends, I had indeed found a peace and acceptance of my own "cancer journey."

She clung tightly, her hand with mine, then softly said, "I'm going to be okay."

At her funeral two months later, I heard her words inside my soul telling me, "I'm okay." I closed my eyes and embraced her spirit. Indeed. You are now cancer free, my dear friend, I thought. One day I will hold your hand again and we'll cry tears of joy, together.

 Psalm 16:5-6, 8
LORD, everything you have given me is good. You have made my life secure. I am pleased with what you have given me. I am happy with what I've received from you. I know the LORD is always with me. He is at my right hand. I will always be secure.

*"It is an endless procession of surprises.
The expected rarely occurs and never in the expected
manner."*

Vernon A. Walters

Chapter Twenty-Two

Lessons from Oil of Olay

I've used Oil of Olay face moisturizer off and on most of my adult life. It was my lotion of choice during the chemo treatments for no other reason than that was what was on my shelf at the time. Each morning before the make-up was put on and each evening after the make-up was cleansed off, I applied the trusty thick, pink Oil of Olay to my face.

At some point after treatments were finished, I switched to something different. It wasn't a conscious decision to switch, just a convenient one; at least I think that was the reasoning.

One evening, more than a year after treatments were finished, I was visiting overnight with my parents at their house in Asheville, North Carolina. I realized that I'd left my current moisturizer at my home. My mom had some Oil of Olay in the guest bathroom I was using, so before I went to bed, I twisted that eloquent black-colored top from its pink soothing bottle and squeezed just a little into my hand.

What happened next took me by complete surprise.

The fragrance of Oil of Olay filled my nostrils like a flower garden, but this flower garden had gone bad. Chemo bad. The smell, that had never been obvious to me before, ran up my nostrils and filled them with dread. Pink was no longer eloquent and soothing. It was hideous and unnerving. Chemo memory dread was smothering me. This subtle fragrance now belonged to chemo and all the associations of that time.

I looked at the mirror and saw myself looking back with a

slightly panicked expression on my face. The moisturizer seeping into my skin didn't appear to be showing any signs of growing warts, turning my skin green, or anything out of the ordinary. This shouldn't be a big deal. Get on with going to bed, I told myself.

I passed my mom in the hallway on the way to my bedroom and paused to say good night to her. She didn't seem to notice the smell as I kissed her goodnight. I lay down in bed in an attempt to fall away to sleep. But the smell wouldn't release me; it was penetrating my entire being. The memories of all those bald-headed nights and anxieties came alive with every inhale my nostrils made even though I resolved this smell would subside. This really shouldn't be a big deal, I thought. What's wrong with me?

Several excruciating minutes passed, and I resolved I wasn't going to win this battle of mind over senses. I bolted up out of the bed, throwing the covers further away than necessary. I was in a fight with an assailant called Olay. I quickly walked down the hallway to the bathroom, hit the light switch with an upward jerk motion, turned on the water faucet with an abrupt twist, grabbed a washcloth, barely waited on the water to warm up, lathered up the cleanser and scrubbed as though I was cleaning tar from my face. Get off—Get off—Get off!

With each rub, I pleaded for the memories to subside. The smell faded, and then disappeared. The memories and anxieties faded too. Crisis passed. I breathed a huge sigh of relief and propped myself up against the bathroom cabinet feeling as exhausted as though I'd just ran a mile.

New lesson. Senses are much to contend with.

Our senses take in much, and remind us of much. I don't eat homemade vegetable soup anymore because that was my meal the night of my first chemo treatment. It was also the one and only meal that I threw up.

One acquaintance told her story of having been served her meals in the hospital on yellow trays. Years later, the illness long gone, she went into a cafeteria where they gave her a yellow serving tray to place her food on. She looked down as she held that tray in her hands. Her hands began to tremble as she released the tray from her grip and ran to the nearest restroom where she promptly threw up. The past had come back to her for an unexpected memory visit by way of a yellow tray.

Do you have a favorite fragrance, clothing, or food you enjoy? If you want to continue using them after the chemo or crisis, consider not creating bad memories during the chemo treatments by avoiding them. It doesn't matter how many years have passed. I, for one, won't ever open another bottle of Oil of Olay.

 *Ephesians 5:2*
Lead a life of love, just as Christ did. He loved us. He gave himself up for us. He was a sweet-smelling offering and sacrifice to God.

*"If I had my life to live over,
I would never have insisted
the car windows be rolled up
on a summer day because
my hair had just been
teased and sprayed."*

Erma Bombeck

Chapter Twenty-Three

How to Go Bald with Eloquence

Realize this may be the hardest part of the whole journey.

Don't say, "I shouldn't feel so sad; it's just hair." Allow yourself to grieve the loss.

Maintain some control. When you run your fingers through your hair and you end up with something in your hand that resembles a small furry cat, it is time to let it go.

Call your favorite hairstylist and let her/him in on your secret, and that your new hairstyle will not involve coloring, highlighting or a perm. Ask for their help.

If you have kids, consider involving them. Let each child have a turn at using the shears, under the CAREFUL guidance of your favorite hairstylist so as not to lose any ears as you lose your locks.

Embrace your reflection in the mirror. Embrace the new you.

Take a friend with you to help pick out a wig; be sure to pick someone who will tell you how great you look.

Buy a good quality wig, one that looks like your normal color and hair. Or, buy a good quality wig that doesn't look like you. Have fun with a different hair color and enjoy confusing the heck out of people.

Wear the wig sparingly at first. It will bother you around the lower edges for a while. Your head is tender there. And don't buy the plastic soft-strap that can help with the wig's seam at your lower head—it's more aggravating than it's worth.

Relish the soothing water from the shower as it massages your head.

Enjoy the extra time you now have getting ready for your day, as it will take half the time it used to.

Try to have fun with the shocked faces of others when they see you for the first time with a new hairstyle.

Wear a pretty hat with a stylish, soft scarf on your head for a different look and comfort.

Smile graciously when the stranger and her daughter come up to you when you are in a card store and ask, "How long?" Let her tell you her success story from her battle that has passed as her daughter beams proudly at her. Notice her hair, all there, shiny and pretty and realize that yours too, will grow back someday.

When the treatments are finished and a short layer of hair begins to peep out, routinely shave the fuzz off the ends. It enhances the growth.

Enjoy your new short hairdo and curls. Soon enough your original hair texture and color will return.

Psalm 147:3

He heals those who have broken hearts. He takes care of their wounds.

*"The gem cannot be polished without friction,
nor man perfected without trials."*

Chinese Proverb

Chapter Twenty-Four

Helping Out

It's not easy being around someone when things are life-threatening and difficult. Here are some thoughts from my experience:

– Don't avoid the "elephant in the room." Ask them how they really are, and be prepared for the hard honesty that may follow.

– Take them books to read that will make them laugh. (*Bald in the Land of Big Hair* was my favorite.)

– Go with them to chemo treatments. Take along a good book, cards, or a project you can work with while sitting there. Most people receiving the treatments take a nap and won't be very engaged with interaction and conversation, but do appreciate the company.

– Take them to normal places they've always enjoyed.

– Let them talk about the cancer, if they choose. As much as they want. And as little.

– Meet them for lunch or dinner during the "good week," which is typically the furthest away from the most recent treatment.

– Drop off a meal for them and their family. Be mindful that spicy foods may not be the best choice.

- Send an uplifting card. Send an uplifting card to other members of the family, too.

- Take the significant other out for coffee to let him or her vent or cry on your shoulder.

- When the bald head appears, acknowledge it. This is the hardest part for the patient, men and women.

- Send a funny card. Laughter truly is the best medicine.

- Join a support group yourself, if this is a close friend or loved one, or go with them to theirs if they are participating in one.

- E-mail. Call. Write. Tweet. Post to their Facebook wall. Hire a plane to drag a banner behind. Whatever it takes. Make sure they know you are out there cheering them on.

- Walk or run in a cancer event to raise money in their honor for the cure. Wear their name on your "In honor of" sheet and pin it on your back. At the American Cancer Society's "Relay for Life" event in your area, place a luminary in the circle with their name on it. Take a picture. Send a card and a copy of the luminary picture and tell them about the event and how it made you feel as you were participating.

- Drop off a personal "thinking of you" gift. An angel that says, "Be healthy" can sit on the shelf and bring a smile to the survivor as they are reminded of your kind visit.

- Don't avoid them - it's not contagious.

- Invite and monetarily sponsor for them a weekend getaway with or without you. If you have a beach or mountain place, offer it.

- Visit with them. If the energy level is low, be willing and okay with doing nothing.

– Give hugs.

– Pray for them. It will do you good, too.

– Ask God and the universe, "why?" then don't necessarily expect an answer.

– Take them to a movie that will make them laugh.

– Take them to a pretty park on a warm day.

– If finances are a struggle for the cancer patient, start a fundraiser on their behalf.

– Whatever you define as "friend" will be tested. Do from your heart as much and as best as you can.

Matthew 25:35-36
I was hungry. And you gave me something to eat. I was thirsty. And you gave me something to drink. I was a stranger and you invited me in.

"The goal is to live a full, productive life
even with all that ambiguity.
No matter what happens,
whether the cancer never flares up again
or whether you die, the important thing is
that the days that you have had
you will have lived."

Gilda Radner

Chapter Twenty-Five

Recurrence

I haven't had one.

Don't want one.

Dread the thought of it.

Just writing the word makes me take deep breaths and feel anxious.

After my diagnosis, and my new knowledge that it could happen to me, I came to fear the recurrence of cancer. I had met young and old who had recurrences. Some after their monumental five-year mark, which is supposed to be the time when you think you've gotten it beat for certain. To think you've made it, then find out it's back has one adjective:

Cruel.

When the treatments are done and over with, life does evolve back to some sense of normalcy. However, a cancer survivor never fully gets away from the dread or fear, subtle though it may be, of a recurrence. That dull ache in my leg? Hmmm, I wonder if it's back?

Ignorance is bliss. Unfortunately, I'm no longer ignorant of cancer or chemo. I now know how my body reacts to chemo, which is not so well. I know, also, the challenge of the treatments, physically and emotionally. I really don't want to do it again. Writing about it even makes me out of sorts. If I think it will happen, if I even let the thought enter my brain, will I somehow make it happen?

I've come to believe in mental exercises. There are testimonies of the young boy who had cancer who pictured the Pac-man character, with its yellow face and wide mouth, going through his body and gobbling up all of the bad cancer cells. And another of a man who was told he would most surely die, and he proceeded to surround himself with laughter, from real people and movies that made him laugh. Both of these people survived their diagnosis of terminal cancers.

I was at high risk for cancer returning in the first few years after treatments. My exercise became that of imagining angel wings. I pictured their soft feathery white wings brushing my body, inside and out. Brushing away all the bad, leaving me caressed and smoothed by their loving touch.

When I reached my five-year mark, I went to my regularly scheduled visit with my primary oncologist. I was told I could choose to keep coming for regular checks on an annual basis, or I could choose to not. Having a doctor visit on a regular basis is like a comfortable security blanket. You have someone to check you from time to time and tell you everything is fine. I held my breath, as I thought of releasing him, my security blanket.

"If I feel I need you in the future, could I get to you quickly?" I asked my doctor. His response was a positive, "Yes." I had his telephone number, and if I saw him at the grocery store, he would acknowledge me and I him.

Yes, I decided, I could let these annual appointments go. As I left, the doctor and I hugged. I thanked him for his God given talents, and for him being in my life. Tears came into my eyes. They were mixed emotion tears. I had arrived where I feared I would not. Alive. Five years later, alive. He had told me at the beginning, "Most women survive this, there is no reason why you shouldn't too." It takes a positive attitude to battle this and most crater holes of life. It also takes an army to help, which for cancer included the doctors and nurses, along with a support group and family and friends.

As I checked out at the front desk, the receptionist looked at my checkout sheet, and then looked at me with glee. "Congratulations!

You've reached your five year mark!" she exclaimed as we high-fived each other. It was indeed, a celebratory moment. It was also a scary moment, walking out and away from my annual visits and the security blanket feeling.

Some people keep going to their doctors forever. Some ladies who've had cancer in one breast, will say, "Take the other one too so I don't have to worry about it." Some focus on exercise, or healthy diets, whatever it takes to ward off the hideous return. I don't worry too much, but, that isn't to say I live believing it can't come back. I meditate, pray, and let the angel wings brush my body as I move forward with each new day gifted to me.

Psalm 100:1-2, 5 (A Psalm for giving thanks)
Shout to the Lord with joy, everyone on earth! Worship the Lord with gladness. Come to him with songs of joy. The Lord is good. His faithful love continues forever. It will last for all time to come.

"Children learn to smile from their parents."

Shinichi Suzuki

Chapter Twenty-Six

Telling Children

How much information is too much information? First and foremost, you know your own child better than anyone, but the age of a child and their personality need to be considered when a crisis hits. How to handle isn't a cookie cutter, one-size-fits-all process. Thankfully, it appears our society has moved beyond hiding it from them. I'm sure my daughter learned valuable lessons from that time in our lives; lessons we would rather have avoided, perhaps, but lessons that provided us with the capability to empathize when others we know are in a crisis, and to learn to rely on God's grace.

One year after my diagnosis, at the beginning of Lindsay's fifth grade year, the treatments completed a few months prior, my hair short but abundant, she had to write a report for her fifth grade project. There were many options for her to write about, and out of all those options, she chose to research cancer. Whether her choice was a conscious or unconscious choice, I'm not certain, but her curiosity appeared to be peaking. This project concerned me with all the knowledge it would give her about the statistics of how many get cancer and how many die. I wondered if it would scare her. She researched with books from her school's library, information found on the internet, and a few print articles I had on the subject. I stayed close by for any assistance she might need as she put her project together. If the information alarmed her, she never once indicated she feared for me or for our family. She received a good grade on the report and proudly exclaimed that news to me and her dad. She brought up no further concerns.

We began a family ritual that fall after the treatments were over that we are faithful to each year. The first Saturday in October, we crawl out of our beds while the stars are still out in the early morning hours. Any other Saturday, Lindsay would fight to stay in bed. For this event she willingly rises at "dark thirty," and we make our way to the center of uptown Charlotte to participate in the "Komen Race for the Cure." At the end of the event, all survivors are given pink balloons, one for each year of survival. As a unified family, we release my balloons to the heavens.

During my fifth year as a survivor, when my daughter was 14, we walked in our friend, Jan's, honor. Two days prior to the walk, Jan, a seven-year survivor, lost her battle to breast cancer. I handed one of my balloons to Lindsay, and said to her, "For Jan, and us." With tears in our eyes, we released our balloons towards heaven and Jan. At the age of 14 she was reminded that death can be part of cancer, and how lucky we are that I'm still here carrying balloons. We marvel together at the number of women carrying fifty helium balloons, and wonder if the balloons will carry them away. There is also the rude reminder that each year there are many women carrying single balloons.

Each year the Komen race is something my daughter is diligent about participating in and while I have treasured our time together as a family, I hope that one day there is a cure for all who suffer. I hope someday we'll have a reason to celebrate NOT needing to participate in this October tradition.

In the fall of 2011, I was part of a select group of breast cancer survivors honored by a group called Focus on a Cure (FOC). Lindsay had already made some plans with friends for the evening of the event, but when I told her about being an honored guest at this fundraiser, she didn't hesitate to cancel her plans. At the fundraiser, all the survivors were asked to share a few words. What I shared was, "we are all survivors of something in life; divorce, death of a loved one; or something else. Ours just happens to be breast cancer. We all face challenges, some large, some small.

Through God's grace and love from family and friends, we find our path to survive." When I returned to my seat, Lindsay reached over and hugged me. "Good job, Mom," she said. "Thank you, sweetie," I answered, and looking at her father sitting beside her, who was smiling in admiration, I added, "I couldn't have survived without you two."

A little while later, a young girl who was about Lindsay's age, made a special trip over to our table. She said, "Thank you for what you said. It was such an inspiration." I was touched that my brief words had affected someone outside of my inner close-knit family circle.

Today, Lindsay lives her life knowledgeable, but without fear of cancer. When I ask her if it bothers her that I had it, she simply shrugs her teenage shoulders, and says, "Not much."

What I do know is, when she goes to the doctor to get her physical, the list of health questions will all be checked "No" except the one: "Family History of Cancer." That box will have to be checked "Yes." I trust her doctors will give her extra care and I hope she'll be proactive about getting her mammograms.

 Romans 5:3-5
We are full of joy even when we suffer. We know that our suffering gives us the strength to go on. The strength to go on produces character. Character produces hope. And hope will never let us down.

*"Hope is a good thing, maybe the best thing,
and no good thing ever dies."*

Shawshank Redemption

Chapter Twenty-Seven

Hope

I sometimes allow my thoughts to journey back in time, to that summer morning when the biopsy results became a crescendo rising to its full pitch that spilled out of the doctor's voice—

"You have cancer."

As the emotional floodwaters rose, I waded into their depths. In disbelief, I felt as though I was watching another person's life play out in front of me. Could this really be happening to me? I was supposed to be smiling, dancing, laughing. Instead, I spent listless days dealing with cancer: ongoing doctor appointments, continuous scans, multiple surgeries. I was riding in a boat of despair and all I wanted was to get off that boat and plant my feet on safe, secure land.

So many things drowned in my life during the treatments: health, energy and once-stupid priorities like having a fancy car and living in the right zip code. Heck, I just wanted to live; I didn't care which zip code. A gift of a new perspective slowly evolved. This new perspective became so important that I risked much when I eventually left the comfortable salaried, (albeit draining) job I was in at the time. Although I needed a salary, I knew I couldn't battle cancer and battle the managers at the same time. I believed there would be a better day, both from cancer and the hideous job. I believed, I anticipated, I hoped. Hope was the anchor keeping my emotional boat from sailing out of port and into oblivion.

My new perspective created new priorities: to reflect more; be more; love more. Things that used to turn on my anger motor, like my adolescent daughter's annoying habits of keeping her room a mess, playing her iPod too loud, rolling her eyes at me when I asked her to do something—don't get me wrong, that was still annoying. But it stopped turning on the anger motor, well, at least not to the decibel levels I had previously allowed it to. I am now simply glad to be in the same room with her, annoying deeds and all. I relish life more. Things like being able to ruffle my dog's thick and soft fluffy fur up around his neck with both my hands as I scrub his chin. Even getting lost on a trip has newfound rewards; the story of being lost will create something interesting to talk about. The aura of a new sunrise, which has always been a wonderful experience, now seems much more profound to me. These new priorities of reflecting, being, and loving are a harmonious path and I feel as though I've launched my boat into calmer waters. While I know a tsunami can always lurk beneath them, I try to stay focused on living in the moment. I don't do this with perfection every day, but I do it a lot better than I used to.

The scripture states "Faith, hope, and love; the greatest of these is love."

I believe these ingredients make a tremendous trio. Is one of these great without the other? To me, the foundation of this trio is faith: A faith in God and living my life in such a way that I'm centered on the fact that whatever comes my way, God will see me through it. Love rounds things out: Love, abides all things, endures all things. Love is great. God's love is greatest. The hope component has been placed strategically between faith and love, bridging the two together. Supporting all. Hope is the critical component. Hope is optimism for a better day. Hope that we can press on even when the doors feel like they are closing tightly in front of us, believing we can endure. We hope for better moments and better days with a faith that God is here beside us and that His love will light the path on which we journey.

What do I have now that I didn't have before the cancer diagnosis? I believe it is this: I've become knowledgeable, but I do not mean in the intellectual sense with all that I've learned about medical terms, the latest drugs, or various cancer statistics. No, I believe what I have gained is a master's degree in living life from the heart. This moment, this day is what we have. Now. Live it with the wisdom that all is indeed a gift.

Reflect.

Be.

Love.

Have faith.

Have hope - in all things.

 1 Corinthians 13:13
The three most important things to have are faith, hope and love. But the greatest of them is love.

My Journey
Carol Fore Injaychock

The news was only three words.
It was a short sentence for something that would change my
life so much.

"How do I begin this journey?" I asked myself.
The answer was, not alone.

There were doctors, nurses, family and friends,
And people I did not know.

As I began my journey, the path seemed dark and dismal.
The supporting words came, the prayers came,
Encouraging me.
I reached within myself to find strength.
Strength I did not know I had, propelling me forward.

Small amounts of power lights began to shine on my journey.
The Power lights had names;
Power of Love; Power of Prayer; Power of Healing;
Power of Inner Strength; Power of God.

Some days were easy.
Most days were not.

When my hair fell out, it felt like my spirit fell out too.
I struggled to continue my journey forward—one foot in
front of the other,
Hoping not to fall;
Hoping to have strength to get back up if I did,

Very unsure of where I was going.
My journey's path eventually became clearer.
The sun began to shine brighter.
My days started to feel warmer.
The strength returned.

I looked in the mirror.
The hair had returned.
But something was gone; my old self was no longer there.
There was instead a new self.

The new self had knowledge I did not have before.
Knowledge that can only come from a dark journey.
A dark journey that taught me what life is really all
about... Living.

Living to Love. Living to Feel. Living to Give.
Living to be the person God intended me to be.

The darkness of the Journey was great.
But the light that shone into the darkness was greater.
That light came from hope and love.

I live today as fully as I can.
Making this day of my life's journey as complete as possible.

I survive each day,
Believing that tomorrow will come.

I look towards the heavens and give thanks.

Afterword

Since Carol's diagnosis, her relationship with God and Christ has strengthened. She continues to serve her home church in a variety of capacities—as a deacon, Sunday school teacher, and committee member with St. John's Baptist Church in Charlotte, N.C. where she has been a member since 1991. After her chemotherapy and radiation treatments ended, Carol left the grocery industry, where she had worked for over 14 years, and began a new career in the financial advisory world, an arena she'd always found interesting. She also renewed her passion for writing, something she had left behind after high school. She had an essay published in the anthology, *Imagining Heaven*, entitled "Finally," and she has written and published numerous devotionals for her church.

Most gratifying of all, she has also mentored others through their own battles with cancer—a testament to her renewed faith, strength, hope and desire to "pay it forward."

Made in the USA
Charleston, SC
27 August 2013